West Virginia University
Morgantown, WV

Written by Matthew Bretzius

Edited by Adam Burns and Kimberly Moore

Layout by Meghan Dowdell

*Additional contributions by Omid Gohari,
Christina Koshzow, Chris Mason, Joey Rahimi,
and Luke Skurman*

ISBN # 1-4274-0218-3
ISSN # 1552-1613
© Copyright 2006 College Prowler
All Rights Reserved
Printed in the U.S.A.
www.collegeprowler.com

Last updated 05/16/06

Special Thanks To: Babs Carryer, Andy Hannah, LaunchCyte, Tim O'Brien, Bob Sehlinger, Thomas Emerson, Andrew Skurman, Barbara Skurman, Bert Mann, Dave Lehman, Daniel Fayock, Chris Babyak, The Donald H. Jones Center for Entrepreneurship, Terry Slease, Jerry McGinnis, Bill Ecenberger, Idie McGinty, Kyle Russell, Jacque Zaremba, Larry Winderbaum, Paul Kelly, Roland Allen, Jon Reider, Team Evankovich, Lauren Varacalli, Abu Noaman, Jason Putorti, Mark Exler, Daniel Steinmeyer, Jared Cohon, Gabriela Oates, David Koegler, and Glen Meakem.

Bounce-Back Team: Chris Fisher, Steve Sinning, and Seth Hall.

College Prowler®
5001 Baum Blvd.
Suite 750
Pittsburgh, PA 15213

Phone: 1-800-290-2682
Fax: 1-800-772-4972
E-Mail: info@collegeprowler.com
Web Site: www.collegeprowler.com

Welcome to College Prowler®

During the writing of College Prowler's guidebooks, we felt it was critical that our content was unbiased and unaffiliated with any college or university. We think it's important that our readers get honest information and a realistic impression of the student opinions on any campus—that's why if any aspect of a particular school is terrible, we (unlike a campus brochure) intend to publish it. While we do keep an eye out for the occasional extremist—the cheerleader or the cynic—we take pride in letting the students tell it like it is. We strive to create a book that's as representative as possible of each particular campus. Our books cover both the good and the bad, and whether the survey responses point to recurring trends or a variation in opinion, these sentiments are directly and proportionally expressed through our guides.

College Prowler guidebooks are in the hands of students throughout the entire process of their creation. Because you can't make student-written guides without the students, we have students at each campus who help write, randomly survey their peers, edit, layout, and perform accuracy checks on every book that we publish. From the very beginning, student writers gather the most up-to-date stats, facts, and inside information on their colleges. They fill each section with student quotes and summarize the findings in editorial reviews. In addition, each school receives a collection of letter grades (A through F) that reflect student opinion and help to represent contentment, prominence, or satisfaction for each of our 20 specific categories. Just as in grade school, the higher the mark the more content, more prominent, or more satisfied the students are with the particular category.

Once a book is written, additional students serve as editors and check for accuracy even more extensively. Our bounce-back team—a group of randomly selected students who have no involvement with the project—are asked to read over the material in order to help ensure that the book accurately expresses every aspect of the university and its students. This same process is applied to the 200-plus schools College Prowler currently covers. Each book is the result of endless student contributions, hundreds of pages of research and writing, and countless hours of hard work. All of this has led to the creation of a student information network that stretches across the nation to every school that we cover. It's no easy accomplishment, but it's the reason that our guides are such a great resource.

When reading our books and looking at our grades, keep in mind that every college is different and that the students who make up each school are not uniform—as a result, it is important to assess schools on a case-by-case basis. Because it's impossible to summarize an entire school with a single number or description, each book provides a dialogue, not a decision, that's made up of 20 different topics and hundreds of student quotes. In the end, we hope that this guide will serve as a valuable tool in your college selection process. Enjoy!

OMID GOHARI ◯ CHRISTINA KOSHZOW ◯ CHRIS MASON ◯ JOEY RAHIMI ◯ LUKE SKURMAN ◯
The College Prowler Team

Table of Contents

Introduction from the Author

Founded in 1867, West Virginia University has been a staple of the state of West Virginia for almost 140 years. WVU completely consumes the city of Morgantown and has slowly become one of the best college towns in the nation. Being one of two major universities in the state, WVU garners much of the in-state enrollment. There are also many out-of-state students that come to WVU each year. WVU is a school on the rise with great standards in academics, athletics, and a great local atmosphere. WVU also has a long standing tradition of being a university that cares about its students and their well-being. With all of the programs and extracurricular activities available for students, WVU offers something for every taste and preference.

When going through my college selection, the choices I made were based on brief college visits, a vast array of information obtained from other people, and university brochures. I attempted to do research, but it is hard to find a resource that focuses on aspects like social scene, athletics, and other minor things the university offers besides academics and tuition. There are certain things that are important to certain people, and I was no different. I wanted a school with a rich athletic tradition, as well as good education programs and a vibrant nightlife. I happened to know a student at WVU already, so luckily, my search was made a little easier. Not everyone has that luxury, though.

In the following pages, I will try to make your research easier by covering every subject a prospective student may want to know about. It is important that future students really know everything a university has to offer, and hopefully this book will do the job. We will look at every topic a student could think of like academics, parties, guys and girls, and facilities. Regular campus literature doesn't give this type of in-depth look at what a college or university is really like. Hopefully, as you read on, you will gain an accurate portrayal of what kind of school West Virginia is and what it has to offer its students.

Matthew Bretzius, Author
West Virginia University

By the Numbers

General Information

West Virginia University
PO Box 6201
President's Office
Morgantown, WV 26506-6201

Control:
Public

Academic Calendar:
Semester

Religious Affiliation:
None

Founded:
1867

Web Site:
www.wvu.edu

Main Phone:
(304) 293-0111

Admissions Phone:
(800) 344-9881

Student Body

**Full-Time
Undergraduates:**
17,614

**Part-Time
Undergraduates:**
1,039

**Total Male
Undergraduates:**
9,962

**Total Female
Undergraduates:**
8,691

Admissions

Overall Acceptance Rate:
89%

Total Applicants:
10,523

Total Acceptances:
9,409

Freshman Enrollment:
4,359

Yield (% of admitted students who actually enroll):
48%

Early Decision Available?
Students can apply and be accepted as early as in their junior year of high school.

Early Action Available?
Not Offered

Regular Decision Deadline:
August 1

Regular Decision Notification:
Rolling

Must-Reply-By Date:
No set date

Transfer Applications Received:
1,538

Transfer Applications Accepted:
1,402

Transfer Students Enrolled:
869

Transfer Application Acceptance Rate:
91%

Common Application Accepted?
Yes, but it is advised to use the application on the Web site.

Supplemental Forms?
Other forms may be needed and are requested on the discretion of the Admissions Office.

Admissions E-Mail:
wvuadmissions@arc.wvu.edu

Admissions Web Site:
admissions.wvu.edu/ undergraduate

SAT I or ACT Required?
Either

First-Year Students Submitting SAT Scores:
48%

SAT I Range (25th–75th Percentile):
980–1160

SAT I Verbal Range (25th–75th Percentile):
480–570

SAT I Math Range (25th–75th Percentile):
500–590

SAT II Requirements for Admissions:
None

Freshman Retention Rate:
79%

Application Fee:
$25

**Top 10% of High
School Class:**
17%

Financial Information

In-State Tuition:
$4,164

Out-of-State Tuition:
$12,874

Room and Board:
$6,144

Books and Supplies:
$800

**Average Need-Based
Financial Aid Package
(including loans, work-study,
grants, and other sources):**
Average packages vary
from student to student as
it is based on a student's
grades, collegiate level,
and dependency on their
parents. For specific quotes,
WVU Financial Aid should be
contacted.

**Students Who Applied for
Financial Aid:**
73%

**Students Who Received
Financial Aid:**
51%

Financial Aid Form Deadline:
February 15

Financial Aid Phone:
(800) 344-9881

Financial Aid E-Mail:
wvuadmissions@arc.wvu.edu

Financial Aid Web Site:
*admissions.wvu.edu/
undergraduate/finaid/
default.asp*

Academics

The Lowdown On...
Academics

Degrees Awarded:

Bachelor

Master

First Professional

Doctorate

Most Popular Majors:

12% Business, Management, Marketing

11% Engineering

11% Liberal Arts and Science

10% Communications and Journalism

8% Social Sciences

Undergraduate Schools:

College of Business and Economics

College of Creative Arts

College of Engineering and Mineral Resources

College of Human Resources and Education

College of Law

Davis College of Agriculture, Forestry and Consumer Sciences

Eberly College of Arts and Sciences

Health Science Programs

(Undergraduate Schools, continued)

Perley Iasaac School of Journalism

School of Physical Education

Full-Time Faculty:
776 members (89%)

Faculty with Terminal Degree:
87%

Student-to-Faculty Ratio:
22:1

Graduation Rates:
Four-Year: 25%
Five-Year: 48%
Six-Year: 54%

Average Course Load

The average course load depends upon each class. Some classes give no outside work and only require students to read out of the text to prepare for lectures. Other classes give strictly out of class work, meaning students need to spend much more time outside of class to prepare for their next class. In most cases, a student should spend at least an hour outside of each class to prepare for the next class.

AP Test Score Requirements

Possible credit and placement for scores of 3, 4, and 5

IB Test Score Requirements

May be used for credit only

Best Places to Study

Blue & Gold Room in Towers, Downtown Library, Evansdale Library, Montainlair

Sample Academic Clubs

Debate Team, Honors Society, Law Club

Did You Know?

WVU offers 52 different minors that students can choose to pursue along with the study of their majors.

WVU is comprised of three different campuses, Downtown Campus, Evansdale Campus, and Health Sciences Campus. **The Downtown Campus is the largest and most popular area**. It is home to the Mountainlair and a large library. Evansdale campus has most of the creative arts, education, and science classes. Students can choose to take classes on any of the campuses, and shuttles are provided to transport students between all three. Dorms are also spread out among the campuses.

Students Speak Out On...
Academics

"The teachers here are pretty much like teachers anywhere. Some are inspirational, some are just okay, and some shouldn't be teaching at all!"

Q "The teachers and **classes are generally interesting**."

Q "For the most part, the teachers are really good. Most like to see students succeed, and **they make an effort to teach the material well**."

Q "Once you start taking classes in your major, it seems the teachers and classes are better. Other times, **it's hit or miss**."

Q "The teachers whom I have had experience with are all very good. Most are concerned with the success of their students and show it by having office hours for help and giving **good feedback on tests and papers**."

Q "I've been lucky to have some **great teachers at WVU**!"

Q "In my experience, the quality of teachers really ranges. There are **some really wonderful teachers who reach out and care** that the students learn the material. There are others who just teach because it's a requirement of being employed at the University."

The College Prowler Take On...
Academics

The academic take at WVU seems to revolve around the teachers. Most students say that with the right teachers, their classes are great and worthwhile. There is not a large personal relationship between students and teachers until the students get into their major core classes. Once a student reaches those courses, the class sizes are usually smaller, which offers a more intimate setting where students can interact with their professor more easily. Students say they get more out of the smaller classes than they do in a class five times the size. Some classes are comprised of 30–40 students, while others are made up of over 200 students. When registering, a student can see what the size of the class and choose which professor they want to take. Teachers in smaller classes are usually more accessible than in larger classes because there aren't as many students fighting for their time. This being said, if a student prefers to have easy access to their professor, it may be smarter for them to try and register for smaller classes.

The workload also varies from class to class, as well as from professor to professor. Some professors prefer to not give any work outside of class and just have the grade depend on a certain number of quizzes and exams. Others would rather give assignments and readings every night and cut down on exams. Generally, the workload is enough that students must put in enough time, or they will not make the grade.

B-

The College Prowler® Grade on
Academics: B-

A high Academics grade generally indicates that professors are knowledgeable, accessible, and genuinely interested in their students' welfare. Other determining factors include class size, how well professors communicate, and whether or not classes are engaging.

Local Atmosphere

The Lowdown On...
Local Atmosphere

Region:
Appalachian

City, State:
Morgantown, West Virginia

Setting:
Urban

Distance from Pittsburgh:
1 hours, 30 minutes

Distance from Charleston:
2 hours, 30 minutes

Points of Interest:
Cooper Rock
Rail Trail
Wharf District

→

Closest Shopping Malls or Plazas:

Morgantown Mall
9500 Mall Rd., Morgantown

Closest Movie Theaters:

Carmike Cinema
9540 Mall Rd., Morgantown
(304) 983-6870

Gluck Theatre
PO Box 6017, Mountainlair
(304) 293-4406

Warner Theater
147 High St., Morgantown
(304) 291-3777

Major Sports Teams:

VU Mountaineers (football and basketball)

WHAM! (semi-pro football team)

Pittsburgh Pirates (baseball)

Pittsburgh Steelers (football)

City Web Sites

www.morgantown.com
www.downtownmorgantown.com
http://morgantown.literati.com

Did You Know?

5 Fun Facts about Morgantown:

- **On home football game days**, Morgantown becomes the most populated city in West Virginia.
- In the early 20th century, Morgantown housed several important facets of the **glass manufacturing industry**.
- The PRT (Personal Rapid Transit—a public transportation system) was built in the 1970s and one of thefew of its kind that continues to run. The **PRT is one of the best kept transit secrets at WVU**.
- *RacerX*, a national dirtbike magazine, was founded in Morgantown.
- The **first pottery plant** was in Morgantown in 1785.

Famous People from Morgantown:

Marc Bulger, Don Knotts, Nick Saban, Jerry West

Students Speak Out On...
Local Atmosphere

"There is almost always a good and upbeat atmosphere around campus, except after a football loss of course."

Q "The local atmosphere is **pretty laid-back**."

Q "**This is strictly a college town**; everything revolves around the University."

Q "It's a fun town with **lots of stuff to do**."

Q "I love the atmosphere here. **Everything you need is within a short walk away**. Plus, there is plenty to do here like nightclubs, the Rec Center, movies, and a lot of restaurants."

Q "It's a fun atmosphere in Morgantown, at least around campus, since **it's mostly college students**. Once you get out further, it becomes more like a normal town."

Q "With almost 20,000 students, it's definitely a big college town, and everything here is focused on the University. **Downtown, there is more of a party atmosphere** because of all the bars and nightclubs. The other two campuses are home to most of the professional students, and it's a whole different atmosphere."

The College Prowler Take On...
Local Atmosphere

It is absolutely evident that Morgantown is a huge college town. Even with a large part of the population being made up of students, Morgantown residents share as much school pride as students do. There is really no separation between students and residents, as they all share the same town, and they all get along together. One of the reasons for such a great atmosphere is the common love students and residents have for West Virginia football. Having no professional sports team in the state, the Mountaineers have brought a great sense of unity to campus. The students are always upbeat, and school spirit is high. It is hard to go throughout the day without hearing a cheer of "Let's Go Mountaineers!" Students are proud to be at West Virginia, and they aren't afraid to show it. Students aren't the only proud ones, as you can see Mountaineer spirit all through town, as well.

In the surrounding town, there is everything that a college student could need. Wal-mart and Kmart are close and offer affordable options for students. Anything a student may need is available such as drug stores, hair care places, and school supplies. Morgantown is also very safe throughout the day and night. There are always police on the streets, whether they are Morgantown police or campus police. The town is well lit, and there is really no unsafe area that students need to avoid. All in all, Morgantown is the perfect place for a college like WVU.

The College Prowler® Grade on

Local Atmosphere: B+

A high Local Atmosphere grade indicates that the area surrounding campus is safe and scenic. Other factors include nearby attractions, proximity to other schools, and the town's attitude toward students.

Safety & Security

The Lowdown On...
Safety & Security

Number of WVU Police:
47 officers at full capacity

Phone:
(304) 293-COPS

Health Services:
Student Health Services at Ruby Memorial Hospital
(304) 293-2311
$10 co-pay

Health Center Office Hours:
Fall and Spring:
8:30 a.m.–5 p.m. Monday–Friday by appointment;

Summer:
8:30 a.m.–4:30 p.m. Monday–Friday by appointment

Basic Services Offered:

Health insurance

Health service

Nonremedial tutoring

Placement service

Women's Center

Campus Safety:

24-hour emergency phones

24-hour foot and vehicle patrols

Controlled dormitory access (key cards, security cards)

Lit pathways

Did You Know?

West Virginia University actually has their **own campus police force**. These are not just security guards, but actual trained policemen used specifically for the West Virginia campuses. This is a key element in keeping WVU as safe as can be.

Students Speak Out On...
Safety & Security

"I don't know much about the safety and security, but since I don't hear a lot of problems concerning the issues, it seems that they are doing a good job."

Q "The security is good, as they are out at night watching the town, and there are **plenty of emergency call-boxes** all over campus."

Q "The University has implemented a system of blue towers placed around campus with buttons on them to connect you to the police. **If there is an emergency, officers are dispatched immediately**. This is reassuring."

Q "**I feel very safe here**. At any given time, there are students walking up and down the streets going to class or to eat."

Q "Campus police are always right around the corner if you need help, though **their main focus seems to be ticketing illegally parked cars**!"

Q "Security on campus is decent. Most of the time, **you will see at least one police car, if not more**."

Q "There are **emergency stations located all over** the place on and off campus for your safety."

The College Prowler Take On...
Safety & Security

Safety and security on campus is definitely something that WVU takes pride in. There is a strong police presence on campus, but not one that overwhelms students and makes them constantly look over their shoulder. If there is any type of emergency, police are quickly dispatched and arrive in a timely manner, giving students a good sense of security. There are also many blue-light emergency phones all over campus, so students have many outlets to contact someone if they do, in fact, need help.

There really is not much of an "off campus" area due to the fact that the surrounding area of Morgantown is really just an extension of the WVU campus. With this in mind, the surrounding area is probably the safest because it is the most popular area of WVU. All of the nightlife occurs here and is definitely kept under control by the authorities. It is very well lit, and there are always people out, so students have no reason to feel unsafe. Traveling to and from parties and events is a low-worry situation for students. Even though the PRT closes at 10 p.m., students are not without a safe way to get back home. There is a bus that runs until 3 a.m. every night from downtown to campus, so students who stay out later can still get home without a problem. Whether it is with the campus police or the buses, WVU makes sure that their students stay safe.

B+

The College Prowler® Grade on

Safety & Security: B+

A high grade in Safety & Security means that students generally feel safe, campus police are visible, blue-light phones and escort services are readily available, and safety precautions are not overly necessary.

Computers

The Lowdown On...
Computers

High-Speed Network?

There are high-speed networks in all the computer labs and libraries on campus. The dorms are also provided with a high-speed network for students living there.

Number of Labs:

There are three actual computer labs, with other computers located in class buildings and the libraries.

Number of Computers:

Approximately 400

Wireless Network?

Yes, many classroom buildings are wireless hotspots. You can also find wireless access in the Mountainlair, Evansdale Library, and Wise Library.

Operating Systems

Mac OS and Windows

Free Software

WVU gives students living in dorms a free network software called ResNet. They also give out Norton AntiVirus to all students with the ResNet CD.

Discounted Software

WVU offers students discounts on all types of software put out by Microsoft. The most common are Windows platforms and Internet browsers.

24-Hour Labs

The labs run on different hours during different times of the semester. At different times throughout the year, both the White Hall computer lab, and the Evansdale computer lab are open 24 hours a day. This is primarily during finals and midterms.

Charge to Print?

The charge to print is six cents per page. Students can pay cash, or pay with money put onto their student ID.

Did You Know?

The **library has laptops that can be issued out to students** to be used in different spots in the building. There is no charge unless they are returned late. This is great for students who want to use a computer while studying.

Students Speak Out On...
Computers

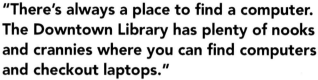

"There's always a place to find a computer. The Downtown Library has plenty of nooks and crannies where you can find computers and checkout laptops."

Q "Computer labs are located in many places on campus. They are usually not crowded, but **the library computers are always being used**."

Q "**There are a lot of computer labs**, but I would still bring my own computer."

Q "I rarely go to the computer labs because I always use my own computer, but when I do go, **I can usually get a computer fairly easily**."

Q "**I recommend bringing your own computer** because a good deal of work is on the computer. Going to a lab whenever you need to do an assignment can be a real hassle."

Q "The computer network on campus is very fast and efficient, but **it has a tendency to shut down on occasion**. Computer labs are equipped with up-to-date computers that run excellently."

Q "**There is a 24-hour computer lab downtown**, which is really nice. The Health Sciences campus library is much smaller, and a computer is hard to find during rush hours, even though it has been expanded."

The College Prowler Take On...
Computers

The computers and computer network at WVU are not lacking. The computers are nothing less than the best technology, and the network is fast and easy to use. There are computer labs located in several different spots on campus—including the library, several classroom buildings, as well as in some of the dorms. Even with all this, it is recommended that students bring their own computers to ensure themselves access anytime they need one. Even with all the computers available, there is no guarantee that a student will find one available every time they may need one. Having one's own computer will also benefit the student who prefers to work later at night, rather than having to squeeze into a 24-hour lab. Not finding a computer is a rare occurrence, but it is still nice for students to have their own.

WVU has mplemented a wireless network in different spots on campus. It has been hooked up in the Mountainlair, as well some class buildings and libraries. When living in a dormitory, students will have to deal with firewalls and Internet regulations set by the University. Students are permitted to use file sharing programs such as Kazaa and Morpheus, but the University does not condone it and sends warnings of consequences for downloading illegal material. Students are not permitted to use online computer video games, however, because it slows down the network for everyone. When living off campus, Internet must be purchased through a local provider. Most are run through cable companies and are very fast and up-to-date. On such networks, students can use the Internet for whatever they want, but they are responsible for their own actions.

The College Prowler® Grade on
Computers: B

A high grade in Computers designates that computer labs are available, the computer network is easily accessible, and the campus' computing technology is up-to-date.

Facilities

The Lowdown On...
Facilities

Student Center:
The Mountainlair is located at the center of the Downtown Campus. It has a food court, huge study area, coffee shop, convenience store, post office, copy center, a bowling alley, and a pool hall. It's also home to Gluck Theatre, and the campus radio station U92.

Libraries:
There are several libraries on both campuses. These include the Downtown Library, Evansdale Library, Health Sciences Library, Law Library, and Math Library. Students can also check out these databases *www.libraries.wvu.edu.*

Athletic Center:
The Student Recreation Center is located on the Evansdale campus. The Rec Center offers basketball, badminton, track, a pool and hot tub, racquetball, squash, multiple weight rooms, and multiple exercise machines. It also houses a rock-climbing wall molded after Coopers Rock, a popular nature spot in the area.

Campus Size:
913 acres

What Is There to Do on Campus?

West Virginia's campus is filled with different things for students to do. One of the most concentrated areas of activity on campus is the Mountatinlair. Students can take a break from work by playing pool or bowling. It's also a great place to grab a cup of coffee or a quick snack. Students can get work done in the study lounge, too.

Movie Theater on Campus?

The Gluck Theatre is located in the Mountainlair. Admission is $3 with free popcorn and soda provided to the students. The Gluck shows movies that just left the theater and are about to come out on video. The Warner Theatre is located at 147 High Street. It offers a discounted admission with a student ID. It has an old-time, traditional look. Both theaters are a five-minute walk from Downtown Campus.

Bowling on Campus?

There is a bowling alley on the bottom floor of the Mountainlair. It offers discount rates for students. It also offers leagues and intramural bowling during the school semesters.

Bar on Campus?

No, but there are over 30 bars within a five-minute walk from the Downtown Campus.

Coffeehouse on Campus?

There are many different coffeehouses within a five-minute walk of the Downtown campus. These are good places to go and relax, or hear live music.

Favorite Things to Do

The bars and clubs are where most college kids can be found at night. The Rec Center is also a very popular area for students any time of day. Another favorite student activity is attending all the different athletic events that occur throughout the year.

Popular Places to Chill

Many of the off-campus bars are popular places to hang out at night. During the day, students hang out at the Mountainlair in between classes. Other hang out spots are the Side Pocket Pub and the Pool Hall in the basement of the Mountainlair. A lot of students are home during the day, but when night comes, the bars and dance clubs become the places to be.

Students Speak Out On...
Facilities

{ **"All of the facilities are well kept and really nice. They take pride here in having a beautiful campus."**

Q "There is a **state-of-the-art rec center** and library. There are also many historical buildings in which classes are held, which are also really nice."

Q "The **Mountainlair is a great student center** providing us with places to socialize, as well as eat and do work."

Q "The athletic facilities, like Milan Puskar Stadium and the Coliseum, are the **perfect venues** for college sporting activities."

Q "The facilities on campus are **always clean and well kept**."

Q "The facilities are really nice. A lot of things have been renovated, so there are more **high-tech facilities and equipment around campus**."

Q "**The Rec Center is one of the best I have ever seen**. The library is also really nice. They kept the original Evansdale Library from when it was first built and added onto it in 2000."

The College Prowler Take On...
Facilities

The facilities on campus truly are state-of-the-art and play a pivotal role in the lives of the students. The best facilities on campus are the Mountainlair and the Student Rec Center. The Mountainlair is truly the definition of a student union, as it has many facets that bring students together. Inside, students can find a food court, bowling alley, pool hall, video arcade, movie theater, and a radio station. There is also a large study area and a wireless hotspot for students that wish to use the building to study. The Rec Center is only a few years old. It offers three new weight rooms, an exercise machine room, five basketball courts, a volleyball court, a badminton court, racquetball and squash, ping pong, swimming, and a rock-climbing wall. Admittance is paid for with a small student fee, and the Rec Center has become one of the most popular places on campus.

WVU has so many great resources that students don't need to travel more than 10 minutes to find anything they need. There are several small convenience stores around campus that can provide students with things they need spur of the moment. Being that the campus is a huge part of town, there isn't really anything that either the campus or town lacks because they are joined together. There are plenty of things to do such as movie theaters and bowling alleys, and bars, shops, and restaurants all within walking distance of either campus. WVU is truly located in a college town, and students can always find everything they need.

The College Prowler® Grade on

Facilities: A-

A high Facilities grade indicates that the campus is aesthetically pleasing and well-maintained; facilities are state-of-the-art, and libraries are exceptional. Other determining factors include the quality of both athletic and student centers and an abundance of things to do on campus.

Campus Dining

The Lowdown On...
Campus Dining

Freshman Meal Plan Requirement?

Yes, for any student living in a West Virginia dormitory.

Meal Plan Average Cost:

Meal plans start at $1,210 per semester, which includes 10 meals a week and go as high as $1,665 per semester, which includes 209 meals per semester and $100 flex money. All meal plans can be seen at *www.sa.wvu.edu/wvudining/mealplans.shtml.*

Places to Grab a Bite with Your Meal Plan:

Dining Halls:
Arnold Café

Location: Arnold Hall

Food: Huge variety; waffles for breakfast, deli for lunch, and pork roast for dinner.

Favorite Dish: Honey-dipped chicken

Hours: Monday–Friday 7 a.m.–9:30 a.m., 11 a.m.–1:30 p.m., 5 p.m.–8 p.m.

Boreman Bistro

Location: Boreman Dormitory

Food: Strictly lunch and dinner during the week, and then brunch and dinner on the weekends

Favorite Dish: Duke of Ribs

Hours: Monday–Friday 11 a.m.–6:30 p.m., Saturday–Sunday 9 a.m.–6:30 p.m.

Café Evansdale Dining Hall

Location: Evansdale Residential Complex (Towers)

Food: There are three lines and a salad bar. One line always has things like hot dogs, hamburgers, and chicken. A second has pizza and spaghetti. The third has a main course that differs every night. Occasionally, there are hot stations out front that have foods like ham and roast turkey.

Favorite Dish: Popcorn chicken, roast turkey

Hours: Monday–Thursday 7 a.m.–8 p.m., Friday 7 a.m.–6:30 p.m., Saturday– Sunday 9 a.m.–6:30 p.m.

Stalnaker Dining Room

Location: Stalnaker

Food: Strictly lunch, dinner, and a snack menu

Favorite Dish: Manicotti

Hours: Monday– Thursday 11 a.m.–8 p.m., Friday 11 a.m.–2 p.m.

Summit Café

Location: Summit Hall

Food: Options include a cereal bar, the Grill, salad bar, a deli, "tastes of home" including three entrees (one vegetarian) and two soups (one vegetarian), daily specials, and a beverage station

Favorite Dish: Nachos Ranchero, and sausage and chicken jambalaya

Hours: Monday–Friday 7 a.m.–7 p.m., Saturday– Sunday 11 a.m.–1 p.m., 4:30–6:30 p.m.

Campus Eateries:

Bits & Bytes

Food: Fresh, made-to-order sandwiches and salads, freshly baked pizzas, snacks, and assorted sodas and coffee

Location: G-69 Engineering Hall

Favorite Dish: Cheese pizza

Hours: Monday–Friday 7:30 a.m.–3:30 p.m.

Brew 'n Gold Café

Food: Starbucks coffee, breakfast items, subs, and sandwiches

Location: Main floor of Braxton Hall

Favorite Dish: Steak sub

Hours: Monday–Friday 7 a.m.–9 p.m.

Fieldcrest Dining Room

Food: Daily selection of "grab 'n go" breakfast items inlcuding cereals, donuts, pastries, bagels, granola bars, fruit, milk, juices, and coffee

Location: Fieldcrest Hall

Favorite Dish: Coffee and pastry

Hours: Monday–Friday 7 a.m.–9:30 a.m.

Freshëns

Food: Variety of smoothies, shakes, and tasty treats.

Location: Mountainlair Food Court

Favorite Dish: Strawberry smoothie

Hours: Monday–Friday 10 a.m.–9 p.m., Saturday 12–9 p.m., Sunday 2–9 p.m.

Hatfields

Food: Breakfast and lunch choices with a regular meal or a "Healthy U" option

Location: Mountainlair Food Court

Favorite Dish: BBQ pork sandwich, salmon salad

Hours: Monday–Friday 7:15–9:15 a.m., 11 a.m.–2 p.m.

Lyon's Den

Food: Freshly baked pizza, made-to-order deli sandwiches, and snacks

Location: Lyon Tower's Main Floor, Evansdale Residential Complex

Favorite Dish: Pepperoni pizza

Hours: Sunday–Thursday 8 p.m.–2 a.m.

McCoy's

Food: New York-style deli, chicken tenders and wings, fries, salads, assorted beverages

Location: Mountainlair Food Court

Favorite Dish: Wings

Hours: Monday–Friday 10 a.m.–6:30

Mean Gene's Burgers

Food: Burgers, fries, assorted beverages and breakfast selections

Location: Mountainlair Food Court

Favorite Dish: Cheeseburger

Hours: Monday–Friday 7:30 a.m.–9 p.m., Saturday 12 p.m.–9 p.m., Sunday 2 p.m. p.m.

Sports Café

Food: Sub sandwiches, salads, snacks, assorted sodas, juices, power drinks, smoothies, and power bars

Location: Student Recreation Center

Favorite Dish: Power drinks

Hours: Monday–Friday 1 p.m.–8:30 p.m. (Closed 4 p.m.–4:30 p.m. daily)

Waterfront Café

Food: Variety of sandwiches and snacks

Location: One Waterfront Place in Morgantown's Wharf District

Favorite Dish: Turkey sandwich and chips

Hours: Monday–Friday 8 a.m.–3 p.m. (Closed 2 p.m.–2:30 p.m. daily)

Off-Campus Places to Use Your Meal Plan

The only places to use the student meal plan that could be considered off campus are the restaurants at the Mountainlair. Inside, students can find a hamburger place called Mean Gene's, a smoothie shop, and a chicken and sub shop called McCoy's. Students can use their meal plans at Mean Gene's for breakfast and dinner, or use their meal plan for McCoy's at dinner only. Each meal consists of a combo meal and is paid for with a swipe of the student ID.

24-Hour On-Campus Eating?

There isn't anywhere on campus where meal plans can be used 24 hours a day, but there are some places open later for students needing a late-night snack. The Lyon's Den is located in the Evansdale Residential Complex and is open until 2 a.m. Students can pay cash, or use any money put onto their ID card. They offer anything from subs and wings, to chips, cookies, or cereal. This is a student favorite for those that live in Towers.

Student Favorites

A favorite place for students to eat at other than a dining hall is Mean Gene's or McCoy's in the Mountainlair. Students can get a combo meal that is deducted right off their meal plan. They offer a fast food menu with burgers, fries, chicken, subs, and salads. They can also get breakfast at Mean Gene's in the form of breakfast sandwiches.

Did You Know?

You can put money on your ID called Mountie Bounty or Meals Plus. This money can be used as flex money if you run out of meals in a week, or if you go to places that don't accept a meal plan like Lyon's Den. You can also use MountieBounty at the bookstore. This can be put on by credit card or check.

Students Speak Out On...
Campus Dining

 "Dorm food . . . eww! It gets pretty bland after a while, but there is usually something worth eating."

Q "The on-campus food **could definitely use some work**."

Q "**It's best to eat at the Mountainlair** if you have time. You can use your meal plan most places. It is good food, unlike the majority of the meals at the dining hall."

Q "The **dining halls are absolutely terrible**. The Mountainlair is pretty good and has good food at McCoy's and Mean Gene's."

Q "Food on campus is not too bad. **Stalnaker has the best food for dining halls**."

Q "The dining hall food is tasty, but it **can get very old after a while**."

Q "Beware of the all-you-can-eat buffets in all the dining halls because **they are the main factor in the Freshman 15**!"

The College Prowler Take On...
Campus Dining

There are certainly a lot of options available for students to use their meal plans, and the food in the dining halls is good, but students grow tired of the never-changing menu after eating the same meal three or four times a week. There aren't really many healthy options being served in campus dining halls besides the salad bar. Even though the dining halls are all-you-can-eat, many students have trouble getting anything down with the lack of variety. The place on campus with the best meal-plan food is the Mountainlair Food Court. Two fast food restaurants that know how to make burgers and fries the right way are located there. Unfortunately, quantities are small, as they do not follow in the all-you-can-eat format of the other dining halls.

The food served by campus dining is not exactly the healthiest option available. They will prepare vegetarian or other special requests, but they don't really go out of their way to provide a better choice for students who may be looking for healthier entrees. Freshmen, as well as anyone else living in dorms, are required to have a meal plan but can pick the smallest one if they feel it will be adequate for their needs. Students can also get Mountie Bounty and Dining Dollars to use at places like McCoy's and Mean Gene's. Although there are so many options for students to choose from, there is not much satisfaction with the dining halls. Eating in the dining halls is something that is not suggested for more than a year if it can be helped. It is definitely worth the hassle of cooking your own meal.

The College Prowler® Grade on
Campus Dining: C

Our grade on Campus Dining addresses the quality of both school-owned dining halls and independent on-campus restaurants as well as the price, availability, and variety of food.

Off-Campus Dining

The Lowdown On...
Off-Campus Dining

Restaurant Prowler:
Popular Places to Eat!

Applebee's

Food: Wide variety; main entrees or burgers and sandwiches

1065 Van Voohris Road

(304) 599-3733

Cool Features: There is a bar area, as well as a restaurant. Offers good happy hour specials.

Price: $18–$20

(Applebee's, continued)

Hours: Sunday 10 a.m.– 11 p.m., Monday–Thursday 11 a.m.–11 p.m.,Friday– Saturday 11 a.m.–12 a.m.

Boston Beanery

Food: Pub food; steaks, chicken, sandwiches, burgers, salads

383 Patteson Drive

(304) 599-1870

Cool Features: Good pub atmosphere, offers signature drinks and party platters; serves food until an hour before closing.

→

(Boston Beanery, continued)

Price: $8–$10

Hours: Sunday–Thursday
11 a.m.–12 a.m., Friday–
Saturday 11 a.m.–1 a.m.

Buffalo Wild Wings (BW3's)

Food: Chicken wings,
sandwiches, burgers

268 High Street

(304) 292-2999

www.buffalowildwings.com.

Cool Features: Great bar

Price: $10–$20

Hours: Sunday 11 a.m.–
1 a.m., Monday–Saturday
11 a.m.–2:30 a.m.

Casa D' Amici

Food: Italian; pizza, subs, rolls

285 High Street

(304) 292-4400

Cool Features: They have
karaoke in the basement
every night.

Price: $7–$15

Hours: Sunday–Tuesday
11 a.m.–1:30 a.m.,
Wednesday–Saturday
11 a.m.–3:30 a.m.

D.P. Dough

Food: Calzones

405 High Street

(304) 292-2444

Cool Features: 40 different
types of calzones

(D.P. Dough, continued)

Price: $8–$15

Hours: Sunday–Tuesday
11 a.m.–2 a.m., Wednesday–
Thursday 11 a.m.–3 a.m.,
Friday–Saturday 11 a.m.–
4 a.m.

Eat'n Park

Food: Diner-type food,
sandwiches, and burgers,
breakfast and brunch

353 Patteson Drive

(304) 598-0020

Cool Features: Open 24 hours
a day, and gives discounts to
students with IDs.

Price: $10–$15

Hours: Daily 24 hours

Gibbie's Pub & Eatery

Food: Pub food; sandwiches,
wings

368 High Street

(304) 296-4427

Cool Features: Karaoke night
on Thursdays.

Price: $10–$15

Hours: Daily 11 a.m.–3 a.m.

The Great Wall

Food: Chinese cuisine

220 High Street

(304) 291-3417

Cool Features: Fortune cookies

Price: $7–$10

Hours: Daily 11 a.m.–11 p.m.

Outback Steakhouse

Food: Grillhouse specials; steaks, chicken, ribs, fish, sandwiches

510 Ventrue Drive

(304) 296-2896

Cool Features: Great steakhouse atmosphere.

Price: $18–$25

Hours: Monday–Thursday 4 p.m.–10 p.m., Friday 4 p.m.–11 p.m., Saturday 3 p.m.–11 p.m., Sunday 12 p.m.–9 p.m.

Panera Bread

Food: Sandwiches, soups, breads, salads, and pastries

357 Patteson Drive

(304) 598-3901

Price: $6–$10

Hours: Daily 7 a.m.–10 p.m.

Rusted Musket

Food: Subs, hoagies, stacker sandwiches

2005 University Avenue

(304) 284-8477

Cool Features: Home of Morgantown original stacker sandwich.

Price: $10–$15

Hours: Sunday–Thursday 12 p.m.–2 a.m., Friday 12 p.m.–3 a.m., Saturday 1 p.m.–3 a.m.

Shoney's

Food: Diner food; entrees, appetizers, salads, sandwiches; breakfast and brunch

3504 Monongahela Boulevard

(304) 599-9606

Cool Features: Lots of food for cheap.

Price: $6–$13

Hours: Daily 6 a.m.–12 a.m.

Texas Roadhouse

Food: Grillhouse specials, steaks, chicken, ribs, fish, sandwiches

3035 Monongahela Boulevard

(304) 598-0109

Cool Features: Great steakhouse atmosphere, and servers do line dances in open spaces.

Price: $18–$25

Hours: Monday–Thursday 4 p.m.–11 p.m., Saturday–Sunday 12 p.m.–11 p.m.

Uno Chicago Grill

Food: Italian; pizza, sandwiches, pasta, seafood, and salads

1085 Van Voohris Road

(304) 599-6191

Cool Features: Great happy hour specials.

Price: $10–$15

Hours: Sunday–Thursday 11 a.m.–11 p.m., Friday–Saturday 11 a.m.–12 a.m.

Best Pizza:
Casa D' Amici

Best Chinese:
The Great Wall

Best Breakfast:
Eat'n Park

Best Wings:
Buffalo Wild Wings

Best Healthy:
Panera Bread

Best Place to Take Your Parents:
Texas Roadhouse

Closest Grocery Stores:
Kroger
Located on Evansdale campus, a 5-minute walk from Towers

Giant Eagle
Located at Mountaineer Mall, a 10-minute drive from Downtown Campus

Other Places to Check Out:
Gumby's
Nick's Canteen
Pargo's

Did You Know?

Places like Casa D' Amici and Eat'n Park are open late and have great prices. Many of these places also have a great bar scene inside where students like to hang out while they eat. **These restaurants are very student oriented** and thrive on mostly student business.

Students Speak Out On...
Off-Campus Dining

"There are tons of places to eat off campus, including any fast food restaurant you can think of, which is perfect for college students."

Q "There are tons of **great restaurants within walking distance** of campus."

Q "There are **a variety of different food places to go** eat off campus, and they are all located nearby, so it's just a short walk away."

Q "Some places to go downtown include **Boston Beanery, Gibbies, Buffalo Wild Wings, and Casa D' Amici.**"

Q "Around town, Casa D' Amici and Gumby's have great pizza and good prices. The food at Gibbie's is pretty good, and it's a fun atmosphere. **Buffalo Wild Wings (BW3's) is probably the best place around.**"

Q "Nick's Canteen, Panera Bread, and the mall food court are **good places to eat off campus.**"

Q "The **nicer restaurants include Texas Roadhouse** and Pargo's, both of which have wonderful food."

The College Prowler Take On...
Off-Campus Dining

With so many different choices all over campus, it would be hard for a student to go hungry. Variety, quality, and reasonable prices will please any college student. Choices range from walk-in pizza places and fast food, to affordable sit down restaurants where a student can get a good meal for a decent price. There are great specials at places like Texas Roadhouse and Gibbie's that offer half-price appetizers and wing specials. Buffalo Wild Wings offers great wing specials, as well.

Most of the restaurants are privately-owned and managed. They are mostly all within walking distance of Downtown Campus and open late for students who have the urge for a snack late. Almost every place offers discounts and specials on each night of the week, while some also offer a discount for showing a student ID. Good places to go with your parents or on a date are Texas Roadhouse, Pargo's, Buffalo Wild Wings, and Uno Chicago Grill. Almost all of the restaurants continue with the town tradition of catering to students, as they offer great student specials and free delivery to students. Students are the main source of business for most of the restaurants here, so they treat the students as well as anyone could ask.

B+

The College Prowler® Grade on

Off-Campus
Dining: B+

A high Off-Campus Dining grade implies that off-campus restaurants are affordable, accessible, and worth visiting. Other factors include the variety of cuisine and the availability of alternative options (vegetarian, vegan, Kosher, etc.).

Campus Housing

The Lowdown On...
Campus Housing

Room Types:
Singles
Doubles
Triples
Suites

Best Dorms:
Stalnaker
Boremen
Towers

Worst Dorms:
Summitt
Arnold

Undergrads Living on Campus:
27%

Number of Dormitories:
11

Housing Offered:
Singles: 24%
Doubles: 42%
Triples/Suites: 34%

➡

Dormitories:

Arnold Hall

Divided into Main and Annex

Total Occupancy: 398

Bathrooms: Community bathrooms on the Annex side, and shared bathrooms between suites on Main side

Coed: Yes

Residents: Freshmen, sophomores, juniors, seniors

Room Types: Single, double, and triple rooms on Annex side; suites have two double rooms and a shared bathroom

Special Features: Dining hall, Academic Resource Center, laundry facilities, and a rec room.

Arnold Apartments

Total Occupancy: 174

Bathrooms: Bathroom in each apartment

Coed: Yes

Residents: Sophomores, juniors, seniors

Room Types: Apartments holding 2-3 students

Special Features: Apartments include bedrooms, kitchenette, and bathroom; Also has air conditioning.

Boreman North

Total Occupancy: 227

Bathrooms: Community bathrooms on each wing

Coed: No, all female

Residents: Freshmen, sophomores, juniors, seniors

Room Types: Single, double, triple

Special Features: Dining hall, academic resource center, multimedia classrooms, kitches, TV lounges, and laundry rooms.

Boreman South

Total Occupancy: 315

Bathrooms: Community

Coed: Yes

Residents: Freshmen, sophomores, juniors, seniors

Room Types: Single, double, double suites

Special Features: Dining hall, academic resource center, multimedia classrooms, kitchens, TV lounges, and laundry rooms; primarily for upper-class students.

Dadisman Hall

Total Occupancy: 355

Bathrooms: Community

Coed: Yes

Residents: Freshmen, sophomores, juniors, seniors

Room Types: Single, double

Special Features: Lounge, laundry rooms, study rooms, a rec room, and is located right behind the Mountainlair.

Evansdale Residential Complex (Towers)

Total Occupancy: 1,336

Bathrooms: Community

Coed: Yes

Residents: Primarily freshmen, some sophomores, juniors, seniors

Room Types: Single, double, and triple

Special Features: All rooms are air conditioned with carpet and laundry rooms on each floor. Includes tennis and basketball courts, post office, bookstore, learning center, computer lab, and classrooms. It is also within walking distance of Milan Puskar Stadium and the Student Rec Center.

Stalknaker Hall

Total Occupancy: 255

Bathrooms: Provided in suites

Coed: Yes

Residents: Freshmen (Honors Program), sophomores, juniors, seniors

Room Types: Suites, lofts

Special Features: Located right behind the Mountainlair; has dining hall inside, as well.

Summit Hall

Total Occupancy: 555

Bathrooms: Provided in suites

Coed: Yes

Residents: Freshmen, sophomores, juniors, seniors

Room Types: Suites

Special Features: Dining hall and is located one block from the Life Sciences Building.

Pierpont Apartments

Total Occupancy: 315

Bathrooms: Provided in suites

Coed: Yes

Residents: Freshmen, sophomores, juniors, seniors

Room Types: Double- and triple-suites

Special Features: Computer lab, fitness room, laundry facilities, five-minute walk from Milan Puskar Stadium and a five-minute walk from Evansdale Campus.

Spruce House

Total Occupancy: 35

Bathrooms: Shared on each wing

Coed: No, all female

Residents: Freshmen, sophomores, juniors, seniors

Room Types: Singles, doubles, triples

Special Features: Study rooms, laundry facilities, and cable TV service.

Sterling Ridge Apartments

Total Occupancy: 220

Bathrooms: 2 per apartment

Coed: Yes

Residents: Freshmen, sophomores, juniors, seniors

Room Types: Four private bedrooms per apartment, plus washer, dryer, kitchen, and common living area

Special Features: Fitness center, computer center, swimming pool, and free parking.

University-Owned Apartments

Arnold Apartments, Pierpoint Apartments, and Sterling Ridge Apartments are all owned by the University. Students must go through the same process to live in University-owned apartments as they would for dormitories. This includes filling out the WVU housing application.

Bed Type
Twin extra-long, 36" x 80"

Cleaning Service?
There is no cleaning service; students are responsible for cleaning up after themselves. Any mess left after moving out will result in a cleaning bill charged to their student account.

You Get
Single bed, study desk, chair, lamp, curtains, phone. Also included is a living area, kitchen, bathroom, recreation facilities, shuttle service, and laundry facilities.

Available for Rent
Mini-refrigerator

Did You Know?

Students can stay on campus for as long as they would like, but **WUV does not offer guaranteed housing after their freshman year**. Most students move off campus after their first or second year to be more independent.

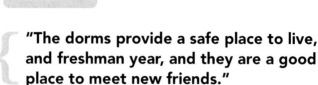

Students Speak Out On...
Campus Housing

{ **"The dorms provide a safe place to live, and freshman year, and they are a good place to meet new friends."**

Q "The dorms are okay except for the food. They are relatively nice; **most rooms are a decent size**."

Q "**Towers is the best place for freshman**, and it's really fun."

Q "**Avoid Summit at all cost**, and Stalnaker is probably the best."

Q "Stalnaker is awesome, and **Towers is too far away**."

Q "Some places to avoid are Summit and Pierpont. **Some of the nicer dorms are Towers, Boreman, and Stalnaker**."

Q "Most freshman live in Towers because it houses many students, making it a **great place to meet people during your first year**. The only downfall of Towers is that it is located on Evansdale campus, which means you need to take the PRT to class everyday."

The College Prowler Take On...
Campus Housing

The dormitories on campus at WVU are in great shape and are excellent places for students to live. Most of the dorms have had recent renovations, including Towers. The University has done a great job maintaining these buildings to provide a good living environment for its students. The rooms are decent sizes, with new bed frames, desks, and dressers provided for the students. The carpets and walls are also in good condition and provide an all around good feel to the dorms. Every room is wired for cable TV and Internet. Some suites may come with kitchen areas and bathrooms, but these options are not available in regular dorm rooms. Every dorm is also located within a five-minute walk from a dining hall, with most dorms having dining halls located somewhere inside the building. Most of the dorms are located on Downtown Campus, but easy transportation is available to students living on other campuses.

Dorm security of the dorms is very good, but it can sometimes be an issue of annoyance with the students. Students are required to present an ID after 9 p.m. in most dorms and can not sign in a guest after midnight on the weekends. Students also are not permitted to sign in a guest of the opposite sex after midnight. Students are only guaranteed housing in a campus dorm for their first year of school. After that, they must go through University Housing and fill out the proper applications in hopes of receiving a dorm room for the following year. The best dorm for freshman is Towers. Other nicer dorms to try for in later years are Stalnaker, Arnold Apartments, and Pierpont Apartments.

B-

The College Prowler® Grade on
Campus Housing: B

A high Campus Housing grade indicates that dorms are clean, well-maintained, and spacious. Other determining factors include variety of dorms, proximity to classes, and social atmosphere.

Off-Campus Housing

The Lowdown On...
Off-Campus Housing

Undergrads in Off-Campus Housing:
73%

Average Rent For:
1BR Apt.: $300–$450
2BR Apt.: $250–$350
3BR Apt.: $250–$300

For Assistance Contact:
Off-Campus Housing Office in Elizabeth Moore Hall

http://studentlife.wvu.edu/ OffCampusHousing/Search

(304) 293-5611

Popular Areas

Grant Street is a popular place to live because it is known as the huge party street. This is where most of the house parties can be found every weekend. It is also popular to live in some of the different apartment complexes near the football stadium because they are the nicest, although also the most expensive. They also offer great opportunities for tailgating and parties for school football games.

Best Time to Look for a Place

The best time to look for a place to live for the following academic year is mid-November to early December. Most landlords like to have their leases signed before the students leave for winter break.

Off-Campus Housing

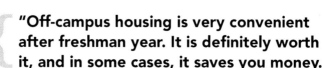

> **"Off-campus housing is very convenient after freshman year. It is definitely worth it, and in some cases, it saves you money."**

Q "It is definitely worth it; do whatever it takes to get out of the dorms! Rent can be pricey, and **apartments range from dumps to new townhouses**."

Q "Off-campus housing is a **good idea if you don't like all the strict dorm rules**."

Q "**It's very worth it and easy to find housing** (though you can't be very picky). Getting out of the dorms is the best decision."

Q "Most people live off campus after their first year. **Start looking early**!"

Q "**Talk to as many people as you can before you sign a lease**. See what your older friends think about their landlords."

Q "There are many places to live off campus because the town is mostly made up of the University. If living off campus, you must be careful that you don't get ripped off. **Look hard for houses that are not run down** or falling apart."

The College Prowler Take On...
Off-Campus Housing

Students are permitted, and even encouraged, to move off campus after their freshman year. As said before, students are only guaranteed space in campus housing for their freshman year, so they could be forced off campus before they graduate if demand exceeds available space. This really is not a problem, however, because there is more than enough off-campus housing to accommodate every student who needs to find a place to live. Almost all off-campus housing is located right on the edge of Downtown Campus in the suburbs of Morgantown, so it is no more than a 15-minute walk to campus each day. There are a good variety of apartment complexes on campus, but most off-campus housing units are full houses, or houses turned into apartments. The prices have been found to be very reasonable, as most rent prices include some, if not all, of the utilities. Living off campus can save students and their families money, as they don't have to buy a meal plan. It has been found that cooking your own food is cheaper than buying a campus meal plan each year.

Traffic both coming in and out of the city is hectic almost all day. The worst times of the day are the morning rush hour and dinner time, when many people are leaving the campus to go home or coming back to Morgantown from work in other areas. Living off campus definitely has its risks, but it grants students more freedom, more room to be themselves, and more opportunity to enjoy their campus experience under their own rules.

B

The College Prowler® Grade on
Off-Campus
Housing: B

A high Campus Housing grade indicates that dorms are clean, well-maintained, and spacious. Other determining factors include variety of dorms, proximity to classes, and social atmosphere.

Diversity

The Lowdown On...
Diversity

Native American:
Less than 1%

African American:
4%

Asian American:
2%

Hispanic:
1%

White:
91%

International:
2%

Out-of-State:
41%

Political Activity

There is not one overwhelming political activity at WVU. There is a Young Democrats club, as well as a Young Republican club. Students are encouraged to get out and vote during elections, whether they affiliate with a particular group or not.

Gay Pride

There is a lot of acceptance of all sexual orientations at WVU. There have been very few issues dealing with hate crimes against homosexual students. There are also several organizations to support gay pride and create a sense of unity among the gay student population.

Most Popular Religions

There is not really a most prominent religion at WVU. In the surrounding area, there are churches for Catholics, Methodists, Presbyterians, and Lutherans, along with Jewish temples. There is a wide variety for students to choose from, so they can go where they feel most comfortable.

Economic Status

West Virginia has been a coal mining state for a very long time. While this is not the wealthiest of areas, they are definitely not the poorest. It is an average economic area, with Morgantown prospering especially because of all the students. There are some poorer areas as the state gets more rural, but for the most part, the state is very industrial and economically sufficient.

Students Speak Out On...
Diversity

"I wouldn't say the campus is very diverse. Perhaps I'm saying this because I don't feel any racial tension on campus, or perhaps there really are not enough minorities to feel any diversity on campus."

Q "I guess it's semi-diverse. **For the most part, it seems mostly Caucasian**, but there is a respectable African American population present, as well as foreign exchange students."

Q "I think the school is **getting more diverse every year**."

Q "I've seen a decent amount of people not from our country, **coming from places such as Africa, India, and Japan**."

Q "I think it is very diverse. There are **a lot of people from foreign countries** here doing research and finishing advanced degrees."

Q "There are **many different types of people** everywhere on campus."

The College Prowler Take On...
Diversity

As can be seen by the statistics, WVU's campus is mostly Caucasian. The gap between the percentages of Caucasians to other ethnic groups is very high. It is clearly noticeable, and students have spoken up about the lack of diversity on campus. There are a few minority clubs around campus, but not very many due to the small number of minority races present on campus. They aren't very visible among campus activities, but that is most likely because the groups are not very large. The tolerance at WVU seems to be at an acceptable level. Complaints about discrimination against race, sexual orientation, and religion have been almost nonexistent. Everyone here seems to accept other people for their differences.

The economic status of the students at WVU varies from person to person. This is definitely not a campus where each student must have the fanciest or most expensive items to fit in with everyone else. Diversity really is not a huge topic among people here at WVU, although the University does have a Diversity Week, which supports several programs and events to promote diversity among different groups. It seems the University is trying to make people aware of different cultures, even if they aren't necessarily present on campus.

The College Prowler® Grade on
Diversity: D

A high grade in Diversity indicates that ethnic minorities and international students have a notable presence on campus and that students of different economic backgrounds, religious beliefs, and sexual preferences are well-represented.

Guys & Girls

The Lowdown On...
Guys & Girls

Men Undergrads:	Women Undergrads:
53%	47%

Birth Control Available?

Birth control and several forms of contraceptives are available through the Student Health Services. Appointments are kept discreet, and prices are a little lower than what a student may pay in a drug store.

Most Prevalent STDs on Campus

Genital Warts, Herpes

Percentage of Students with an STD

1 out of every 8 students

Social Scene

The social scene at WVU is very strong. West Virginia is known as being a party school, and it absolutely lives up to its reputation. There are numerous activities to participate in, and a large population of the University takes part in them.

Hookups or Relationships?

There is a high number of hookups and relationships going on at WVU. There are some people that "aren't ready" for a relationship and would just rather hook up with people without the commitment. Then, there are people who are looking for a relationship and the commitment that comes with it. No matter what you are seeking, you can find it at WVU.

Best Place to Meet Guys/Girls

You can meet guys or girls pretty much anywhere, if you are actually looking for them. Probably the easiest place to meet a member of the opposite sex is at a bar or at a party because everyone is out with the same intent to have a good time and meet some good people. Other good spots are at football games and in your classes, where you're sure to find someone you like.

Did You Know?

Top Three Places to Find Hotties:

1. Bars
2. Parties
3. Classes

Top Five Places to Hook Up:

1. Frat Parties
2. House Parties
3. Dance Clubs
4. Dorms
5. Sorority Parties

Dress Code

There is no dress code at WVU. Every student is free to dress in whatever they feel comfortable in. Whether more proper or casual, many different types of dress can be seen throughout campus. When going out, students try to dress in whatever they think will make them look the best and raise their odds of meeting people of the opposite sex. Girls and guys usually save their most attractive clothes for when they go out on the town.

Students Speak Out On...
Guys & Girls

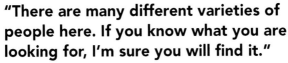

> **"There are many different varieties of people here. If you know what you are looking for, I'm sure you will find it."**

Q "There's a **very nice population of guys on campus**, and yes, they are hot."

Q "The girls and the guys are pretty equal; **some are hot**."

Q "There are generally good-looking girls, and there is really **a lot of different girls to choose from**."

Q "There are a lot of good-looking people here. Let's just say **I'm not complaining about the scenery**!"

Q "There are so many different types of people here that **there is someone for everyone**."

Q "**Guys here are average**, yet plentiful."

The College Prowler Take On...
Guys & Girls

The social scene on campus is very strong. Students at WVU are both socially and academically minded. They work hard during the day and party harder at night. One thing to remember is there are rules in the dorms about having members of the opposite sex in your room. During the day, anyone can be in the dorms, but during the evening, the rules become more strict. Members of the opposite sex cannot be signed in after midnight, and students are not permitted to have members of the opposite sex stay the night in their room. No one actually goes room to room checking for this rule violation, but it will be enforced if it happens to be noticed.

It seems that there is a steady mix of both relationships and hookups. It is common for lot of relationships to start from people just hooking up and developing into something more serious. There is a mix between promiscuous students and people who are a little more reserved on campus. The ratio of males to females is almost even, so competition is minimal for the sexes. There is usually an even distribution of guys and girls at all the social events. Some parties and events can get pretty wild, but other bars and clubs have a tamer atmosphere. The campus does try to promote safe sex as much as possible. They offer free HIV tests, as well as discounted contraceptives in a discreet manor. There are also STD screens and counseling that is provided at the Student Health Center.

The College Prowler® Grade on
Guys: B

A high grade for Guys indicates that the male population on campus is attractive, smart, friendly, and engaging, and that the school has a decent ratio of guys to girls.

The College Prowler® Grade on
Girls: A-

A high grade for Girls not only implies that the women on campus are attractive, smart, friendly, and engaging, but also that there is a fair ratio of girls to guys.

Athletics

The Lowdown On...
Athletics

Athletic Division:
Division I

Conference:
Big East Conference

School Mascot:
Mountaineer

**Males Playing
Varsity Sports:**
301 (3%)

**Females Playing
Varsity Sports:**
193 (3%)

➡

Men's Varsity Sports:

Baseball

Basketball

Football

Rifelry

Soccer

Swimming & Diving

Wrestling

Women's Varsity Sports:

Basketball

Crew

Cross-Country

Gymnastics

Rifelry

Soccer

Swimming & Diving

Tennis

Track & Field (Indoor and Outdoor)

Volleyball

Club Sports:

Archery

Badminton

Crew

Cycling

Equestrian

Fencing

Ice Hockey

Lacrosse

Martial Arts

Raquetball

Rugby

Skiing

Snowboard

Table Tennis

Tae Kwon Do

Ultimate Frisbee

Whitewater Rafting

Intramurals:

Basketball

Bowling

Flag Football

Indoor Soccer

Softball

Tennis

Athletic Fields

Milan Puskar Stadium (football), the Coliseum (basketball), S.J. Diesk Field (soccer), Hawley Field (baseball)

Getting Tickets

Student tickets to sporting events are included in the student activities fee. Students get their tickets through *www.wvugame.com*. Non-students can get tickets from there also.

Most Popular Sports

Football and basketball are the most popular sports at WVU. The student sections are always packed and rowdy for each home game.

Overlooked Teams

Women's and men's soccer and men's wrestling are both overlooked. Each year, they all perform well enough to get into their respective league tournaments. They have also received invitations to national tournaments, as well as had individual players win national honors.

Best Place to Take a Walk

The Rail Trail is a popular place for people to walk and jog. It runs by the river and is often crowded with people. Students can also be seen just walking through campus because it is very well lit and safe.

Gyms/Facilities

The football team has its own training facility in the stadium. The gym for students can be found in the Student Rec Center, which boasts state-of-the-art equipment. It hosts a guy's gym, a girl's gym, and a coed gym, as well as a room filled with exercise machines.

Students Speak Out On...
Athletics

{ **"There are a lot of intramural sports you can sign up for at the Rec center."**

Q "Let's **go Mountaineers**!"

Q "**Varsity sports are very big at WVU**. The football and basketball teams bring in the largest number of fans, but many other sports are fun to attend also."

Q "Needless to say, **WVU football is the biggest** campus varsity sport."

Q "Mountaineer **football reigns supreme**!"

Q "I like the football games because **everyone is having fun and drinking**."

Q "Sports are huge here. Football games are the biggest thing in the state. **Intramural sports are available, but they aren't overly huge**."

The College Prowler Take On...
Athletics

Sports garner a lot of attention and love from not only the students at WVU, but the surrounding community members, as well. There are no professional sports teams in the state of West Virginia, so the Mountaineers are the next best thing. Fan support for the University's athletic teams is extremely high, and the students take as much pride in the teams as the players do. The most popular sports are football, men's basketball, and women's basketball. Football games are almost always sold out on Saturdays, and the Coliseum is always packed for Mountaineer basketball games.

With a new ticketing system, tickets are not as easy to get as they used to be. It is all done online, and students have to request a ticket and then hope to receive an e-mail after a waiting period to find out if they obtained a ticket or not. Student tickets to all athletic events are free because a minimal price is paid in the Student Activities Fee. On football game days, Morgantown becomes the most populated city in the state because of the fan base that travels to Milan Puskar Stadium for the game. Traffic is not as terrible as some would think, however, because the state troopers direct traffic and turn off traffic lights. The best rivalry we have is against the Pittsburgh Panthers. Intramural sports are popular at WVU, but not overly anticipated. There are several sports offered in male, female, and coed leagues during all seasons of the year. The most popular intramurals are basketball and flag football.

B+

The College Prowler® Grade on
Athletics: B+

A high grade in Athletics indicates that students have school spirit, that sports programs are respected, that games are well-attended, and that intramurals are a prominent part of student life.

Nightlife

The Lowdown On...
Nightlife

Club and Bar Prowler:
Popular Nightlife Spots!

Club Crawler:
Chasers & Dreams

376 1/2 High Street

(304) 284-9969

Located between Fayette Street and Wall Street, this club is 18 to enter, 21 to drink. It has a large dance floor, and is deemed a private club.

Chic-n-Bones Rhythm Cafe

444 Chestnut Street

(304) 291-5060

Open from Monday–Saturday. DJ on Thursdays–Saturdays. It's a 21-and-over rhythm club with a dance floor and a full dining menu. Daily specials such as 2 for 1 drinks and half-price appetizers on Wednesday, 25 cent drafts on Thursday, and $2.50 Coronas on Friday nights. Saturday is karaoke night, starting at 10 p.m.

→

Elements

444 Chestut Street, Suite B

(304) 296-5848

Elements has an urban dance club atmosphere. Admission is 18 to enter, 21 to drink. Wednesday has a live DJ, Thursday is college appreciation night, and ladies have no cover and drink for free from 9 p.m.– 11 p.m., Saturdays features happy hour until 11 p.m. with $1 select drinks.

Pulse

2 Wall Street

(304) 225-9500

This is the ultimate dance and hip-hop club for those 21 and over. When the dance-club-turned-concert-venue tried out its first big act, it was just like a smaller, Morgantown version of the Peach Pit After Dark from *Beverly Hills 90210*. But now that it's been there, it's a very big hang out for students.

Vice Versa

335 High Street

(304) 292-2010

Hottest gay club around, Vice Versa has karaoke on Sunday nights, no cover Thursdays, and a drag show on Fridays. Open after 8 p.m. Thursday–Sunday.

Bar Prowler:

Back Door

485 High Street

(304) 292-5936

Slogan is "When it rains, we pour!" Open Monday–Saturday. Daily specials, including Thursday no cover for the ladies until midnight, and bring any cup up to 32 ounce and get $1 drafts. Friday has an all-you-can-eat buffet, and Wednesday is karaoke night.

Big Times

327 High Street

(304) 296-2666

Big Times has a sports bar atmosphere complete with pool tables and poker machines. Must be 21 or over to enter. Daily specials in addition to $4 Jager bombs and $2 domestic bottles.

Fins Beach Bar

491 High Street

(304) 225-3900

Open Tuesday–Saturday, this bar has a beach atmosphere. Great specials, including 50 cent select drinks on Tuesdays, and a 2 for 1 deal on Wednesdays from 9 p.m.–11 p.m. On Thursday's, ladies have no cover, and $3.50 bomb drinks on the weekend.

Lazy Lizard

345 High Street

(304) 296-0004

Motto is they're "Always pouring with a heavy hand." They feature local bands, as well as DJs, and have a large dance floor. They also have a full menu. Over 21 club.

Shooters Lounge

233 Walnut Street

(304) 292-9052

Open 365 days a year, Shooters has a dance floor, live DJs, and pool tables. 18 and over to enter, 21 to drink. This is a place students like to frequent during the week, as well as the weekend.

Bars Close At:

2 a.m.

Student Favorites:

Elements

Lazy Lizard

Pulse

Favorite Drinking Games:

Beer Pong

Card Games (A$$hole)

Flip Cup

Quarters

Power Hour

Primary Areas with Nightlife

High Street is the place to check out when looking for the bars and night clubs. Bars and clubs line both sides of the street and are very popular with students, especially when the weather gets cold. All of the nightlife can be found around the Downtown campus. Grant Street is where most of the house parties can be found. Pretty much only college students live there, so a party can be found every night of the week.

Cheapest Place to Get a Drink

Almost every bar has a Friday night "Drink Til You Drown" special in which students pay $5 at the door and drink on the house until midnight. Besides that, the cheapest place to get a drink is Pulse or Club Z as they are always running great specials on beer and mixed drinks.

Other Places to Check Out

Frat Row is always a decent place to check out on the weekends if you can't find much else to do. Admission for females is usually free, while males pay $5. Once inside, beer is free, and there are usually shots that can be purchased. These are usually very overcrowded and dull for those that are not frat brothers, but it is a good place to meet members of the opposite sex.

Also, check out the clubs/bars Club Z, Levels High Street Grill, and Keglers Sports Bar & Lounge.

Useful Resources for Nightlife

The Sunnyside Superette and the Den are good places to buy cheap beer for any night's festivities. The PRT and drunk bus are also two things to take advantage of when going out on the tow; they are free transportation that prevents drunk driving.

Local Specialties

Creek Water: Vodka, grain alcohol, lemonade and Sprite mixed together. It is usually made in large quantities as a party drink and is preferred by females because of the softer taste.

Moonshine: This is as close to pure alcohol as you can get. Only weaker varieties can be found in stores because it can be very dangerous. It is also more of a folk drink associated with people that live in the hills of West Virginia.

What to Do if You're Not 21

There are plenty of activities to take part in if students are not 21. They can still go to dance clubs and bars and just hang out and meet new people. There is also "Up All Night" at the Mountainlair, which provides free food and fun activities on weekends for students that do not wish to go out to other places. The bowling alley and pool hall in the Mountainlair offer specials to students on the weekends.

Organization Parties

Certain organizations will throw party for their members. Usually different majors, like the law school or the forensics students, participate in organizational parties. Sometimes, University organizations throw game-watching parties for the Super Bowl or WVU football games at the Mountainlair with free food and big screen TVs. Students can always find out about these events through flyers and e-mails in their campus e-mail accounts.

Students Speak Out On...
Nightlife

> **"Parties on campus can vary depending on where you go. Fraternities have large parties that are loud and have lots of people. Some other parties are low-key and usually at houses off campus."**

Q "**There are a lot of bars and clubs on campus** that have deals on certain nights for drinks. This attracts a lot of students due to reasonable prices."

Q "The best bar is Lazy Lizard if you are over 21. **If you are under 21, you can go to Shooters Lounge**, Pulse, and Elements."

Q "Flyers for different bars, clubs, and house parties are commonplace. **Parties are pretty crowded**, so check them out once and see what its like. It can't hurt to BYOB!"

Q "On any given day and especially on the weekend, there are **tons of house parties downtown**. You can just walk down Grant Street and count all the house parties."

Q "There are **a lot of bars and nightclubs** like Shooters Lounge, Keglers Sports Bar & Lounge, and Levels High Street Grill."

Q "**There is always a party to go to any day of the week**, and once is starts getting cold out, you can find everyone at the bars and clubs."

The College Prowler Take On...
Nightlife

The nightlife at WVU comes with such a large variety that students never have to do the same thing twice. For starters, there is the University-sponsored "Up All Night" at the Mountainlair. They offer programs like casino night, movies, crafts, karaoke, free food, and other fun stuff to do on weekend nights. There are also University-sponsored concerts. A lot of the nightlife takes place downtown, where it is more commercialized. There are many shops along the downtown strip, and a mall about 15 minutes away with a movie theater is popular with students. Downtown is also filled with several dance clubs; these are extremely popular with the female population because of great drink specials and large dance floors.

For those students who want to drink, there is a good selection of bars with great drink specials nearby. Some students would rather go to house parties instead of bars and clubs, and WVU will not disappoint in that area. There is always a party somewhere on campus every night of the week. Even for those students who do not want to drink, house parties are great places to meet new people and have some fun being out with friends. Unless a party becomes over-crowded or runs into the street, the police pretty much let them go and just make sure they stay under control. The Student Rec Center also rents out camping equipment at low prices to students, and there are a several great campgrounds in the area. Weekends also provide an opportune time to go to club sporting events.

The College Prowler® Grade on
Nightlife: A

A high grade in Nightlife indicates that there are many bars and clubs in the area that are easily accessible and affordable. Other determining factors include the number of options for the under-21 crowd and the prevalence of house parties.

Greek Life

The Lowdown On...
Greek Life

Number of Fraternities:
14

Undergrad Men in Fraternities:
5%

Number of Sororities:
11

Undergrad Women in Sororities:
5%

→

Fraternities:

Alpha Gamma Rho
Alpha Phi Alpha
Beta Theta Pi
Delta Tau Delta
Iota Phi Theta
Kappa Alpha
Phi Delta Theta
Phi Gamma Delta
Phi Kappa Psi
Phi Sigma Kappa
Sigma Chi
Sigma Phi Epsilon
Tau Kappa Epsilon
Theta Chi

Sororities:

Alpha Kappa Alpha
Alpha Omicron Pi
Alpha Phi
Alpha Xi Delta
Chi Omega
Delta Gamma
Delta Sigma Theta
Kappa Kappa Gamma
Pi Beta Phi
Sigma Kappa
Zeta Phi Beta

Other Greek Organizations:

Greek Council
Greek Peer Advisors
Interfraternity Council
Order of Omega
Panhellenic Council

Did You Know?

WVU has a Web site dedicated to Greek life. It gives information on all the fraternities and sororities, as well as the student government and student organization services. Check it out at *www.wvu.edu/~greek.*

Students Speak Out On...
Greek Life

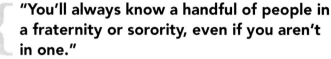

{ **"You'll always know a handful of people in a fraternity or sorority, even if you aren't in one."**

Q "Greek like is **not particularly dominant**."

Q "It does not take over the social scene, but **it is noisy**."

Q "**I would never go Greek** because I would not like to be hazed."

Q "**There is a lot of Greek life here**, if that is what you are interested in, but you can also have a great time and do plenty of other things, if you would rather."

Q "They claim it doesn't dominate, but it kind of does. The **Greek scene is pretty big, and they have decent parties**, if you are into that whole scene."

Q "**Greek life is pretty large at WVU**, but it doesn't overtake the school."

The College Prowler Take On...
Greek Life

There is a good amount of fraternities and sororities on campus, but they do not play a huge role in the social scene. These organizations are only really important to the people that are in them, causing in an inadvertent separation between Greek members and non-Greek members. This being said, fraternities and sororities are a great way to meet new friends, but they are not completely necessary to fit in. Fraternities and sororities also throw a lot of functions and parties. The formals are just for members of the organizations, but they throw many parties that are open to all. These usually cost $5 to get in and have kegs placed throughout the house. Students don't have to be members of the organizations to find out about the parties—they are often advertised so members can make money.

There are a few different opinions of Greek students from non-Greek students. Some think Greek students feel they are better than everyone else, while others just don't care for the whole idea of fraternities or sororities at all. Other students like these organizations because they throw good parties or help them make new friends. If there is one thing the Greek organizations at WVU do extremely well, it's give back to the community. They host more than their share of charitable events, clothing drives, and raffles to help organizations and people in need. While WVU Greek students may not dominate the campus, they do help dominate where it counts, and that is in the community.

B+

The College Prowler® Grade on

Greek Life: B+

A high grade in Greek Life indicates that sororities and fraternities are not only present, but also active on campus. Other determining factors include the variety of houses available and the respect the Greek community receives from the rest of the campus.

Drug Scene

The Lowdown On...
Drug Scene

Most Prevalent Drugs on Campus:
Marijuana is most prominent; ecstasy is close behind it.

Liquor-Related Referrals:
483

Drug-Related Referrals:
16

Liquor-Related Arrests:
356

Drug-Related Arrests:
67

Drug Counseling Programs:
The Student Assistance Program offers counseling programs for not only drugs, but also alcohol and other problems a student may have trouble with. The SAP can be reached through Student Health Services, and appointments can be made over the phone.

Students Speak Out On...
Drug Scene

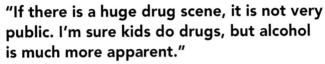

"If there is a huge drug scene, it is not very public. I'm sure kids do drugs, but alcohol is much more apparent."

Q "It seems that **most people stick to alcohol**."

Q "**It's not a big thing around here**. Of course, there's a lot of drinking going on here, but that is all I hear about."

Q "I don't really know how many people use drugs around here. **It's not really public knowledge**."

Q "The drug scene **does not really concern me**, but I am aware that people do them."

Q "**Drugs are readily available**, and they can be easy to acquire if one puts effort into it."

Q "Drugs are probably a problem that isn't very public because **people aren't getting caught very much**. I'm sure a lot of kids do them, though."

The College Prowler Take On...
Drug Scene

The drug scene at WVU seems to be almost nonexistent to the public eye. It can't be said that students definitely aren't using drugs, but if they are, it is not made public knowledge. The substance that is most abused on campus is alcohol. Alcohol is easy to access, and students take advantage of it, sometimes taking it too far. There is alcohol at almost every party, and of course in the bars. Tobacco is seen in abundance, too, as more and more students are smoking each day. Whether it is because of peer pressure or personal choice, cigarette use is popular among students. Campus police say that the most common drug is marijuana; it is allegedly the cheapest and easiest to use. The students that are using marijuana seem to be doing it in the privacy of their own home because it is not seen very often around campus. The same can be said for harder drugs, which are not seen at all in public.

There is always a chance for peer pressure, but there is enough of a non-using student body that students can feel comfortable saying no. The majority of the students do not seem to be abusing drugs, so students should not feel embarrassed for saying no to peer pressure. Overall, the drug scene is not very prevalent at WVU, even with some minor alcohol abuse.

B-

The College Prowler® Grade on
Drug Scene: B-

A high grade in the Drug Scene indicates that drugs are not a noticeable part of campus life; drug use is not visible, and no pressure to use them seems to exist.

Campus Strictness

The Lowdown On...
Campus Strictness

What Are You Most Likely to Get Caught Doing on Campus?

- Drinking or smoking in the dorms
- Theft from dorms
- Underage drinking in clubs
- Cheating in class

www.collegeprowler.com

CAMPUS STRICTNESS | 77

Students Speak Out On...
Campus Strictness

"Be careful what you do in the dorms because someone always finds out. The police will come knocking and will throw you out, put you on probation, or whatever else they see fit."

Q "**You are often found guilty** just because you are a student. They don't really care what you have to say."

Q "Police pretty much let **you have your fun, as long as you don't start trouble**. Stay off the street if you are at a house party, and you will be pretty safe."

Q "**Campus police are not overly strict about parties**. If there is a party that is out of control, they will take care of it, but if it is controlled, then they will let it go."

Q "The police **can't be too strict** because everybody is drinking."

Q "I've never had a run-in with campus police regarding drugs and drinking, so I'm not really sure, but I think they try to crack down on underage drinking a lot. I do know that **they are big on parking violations**."

Q "**They really don't care that much**. They give you rides home and take pictures with you when you do get written up."

The College Prowler Take On...
Campus Strictness

The police presence on campus is very strong, but not completely overwhelming to students. If anything, it gives the students a sense of security knowing that there is usually an officer somewhere in the vicinity. Campus police aren't considered extremely strict, but do they take their stand on some issues. Underage drinking on campus is not something that students want to get caught going—it will result in a citation and possible notification of parents. Other things taken seriously on campus are parking violations. Parking is extremely limited, so those parking without proper permits are given tickets until their vehicle is moved. Dorm violations can also result in probation from student events, removal from the dorm, or even expulsion.

The local police presence is just as strong as the campus police, as they pretty much share duties. While both police forces are very friendly, local police are a little more strict than campus police. It is usually the local police that watch over parties, and they make sure things do not get out of hand. Students usually won't get in trouble for something off campus unless they go looking for it. Neither police force goes out of their way to bust students or cause trouble, but they will go through with their duty and take care of any problems they see fit. What students should definitely avoid doing is drinking or drugs in the dorm. Being caught for either can result in removal from the dorms, or even expulsion, as well as counseling programs and parent notification. Other than that, students are mostly able to come and go as they please, as long as they don't go out of their way to make trouble.

B-

The College Prowler® Grade on
Campus Strictness: B

A high Campus Strictness grade implies an overall lenient atmosphere; police and RAs are fairly tolerant, and the administration's rules are flexible.

Parking

The Lowdown On...
Parking

Approximate Parking Permit Cost:

Parking permits for University lots cost between $100–$175 for a year-long pass.

Parking permits on certain streets for a year-long pass are $5, but doesn't guarantee a spot.

Student Parking Lot?

There are several parking lots throughout campus for students to park in, but most require a WVU parking permit specific to that certain lot. Students can park for free at the Coliseum, but they can not leave their cars there overnight.

Freshmen Allowed to Park?

Freshman are allowed to bring their cars but are encouraged not to because there are not many parking spots.

Common Parking Tickets:

Expired Meter: $10
No Parking Zone: $10*
Handicapped Zone: $10*
Fire Lane: $10*
* And possible tow.

WVU Parking Services:

West Virginia University Parking Office
University Service Center
3040 University Avenue, Room 3304
PO Box 6561
Morgantown, WV 26505-6561
(304) 293-5502

Parking Permits:

Parking permits are needed to park in any University-sponsored lot. They are eligible for use during the entire academic year and can be purchased at the WVU Parking Services office. One permit does not work for all lots, however, so you are only legally allowed to park in the lot you choose to purchase a permit for. Parking in any other lot leaves you responsible and open to tickets or towing.

Did You Know?

Best Places to Find a Parking Spot

Spots on the side of the street like on High Street are usually available. These are all meter spots. There are also several meter lots near High Street that are often available.

Good Luck Getting a Parking Spot Here

One of the hardest places to find a spot is in the Mountainlair during the day. It is filled with cars of commuters and professors, and it's almost impossible to get into unless you are there very early.

Students Speak Out On...
Parking

"You should definitely leave your car at home because parking here is a hassle."

Q "**Parking is very competitive**. There are many parking garages, but you must pay for them. If you don't have a permit, you will most likely be getting a $10 ticket."

Q "Parking is a nightmare. Finding a spot is almost impossible, even though they **added a lot at the intersection of Falling Run Road** and University Avenue."

Q "Parking is a big concern for students. **Parking at the WVU Coliseum is free**, but you can't park there overnight. Yet, Morgantown's public transportation is free for students."

Q "**The city loves to tow cars**, and they do so all the time. I think that's where they get most of their money. They ticket and tow like crazy here."

Q "**Don't bring your car here** unless you plan on bringing enough pocket change to get you through four years."

Q "**You can purchase a parking pass for a hefty fee** on every campus but Downtown Campus, and there are lots of parking garages."

The College Prowler Take On...
Parking

All students are permitted to bring cars to WVU, but freshmen are encouraged to leave cars at home unless they are of absolute necessity. All students who do bring automobiles are required to purchase a parking pass. Permits can cost anywhere from $100–$175 for University-sponsored lots. Students living off campus can buy street permits for $5 for the year, but they do not guarantee a spot. Parking is extremely limited both on campus and in town: Parking anywhere on Downtown Campus is virtually impossible unless students arrive extremely early in the morning to find a spot in the Mountainlair Parking Garage, and there are few meter spots on campus. Parking in town is a little easier than on campus, but it's still few and far between. Mostly all the parking consists of meter spots on the street, or meter lots on side streets.

It is worth bringing a car to campus if students live far away from WVU. That makes it easier on parents who have to pick up their students for vacations. Also, it makes it easier to get to places like the Rec Center, or the mall because students don't have to wait for public transportation. It is always good to have a car to rely on in case emergencies or if public transportation is not running with a student's schedule. It is advised to carpool and only bring a car if it is a necessity. Parking will be a hassle, so students should be prepared to deal with a little stress.

The College Prowler® Grade on

Parking: D

A high grade in this section indicates that parking is both available and affordable, and that parking enforcement isn't overly severe.

The Lowdown On...
Transportation

Ways to Get Around Town:

On Campus

The easiest way to get from campus to campus is the Personal Rapid Transit (PRT). This is a monorail system that runs from the Downtown Campus to Evansdale campus, as well as to the Health Center. It is free to ride for students with the swipe of their ID, and it has great hours through the day. There are also two bus services that run through campus.

The Mountainline is a bus service that runs from campus to campus, as well as to the malls and several other surrounding areas. The University bus system runs from campus to campus; it provides students with a safe ride home from downtown after the PRT has closed.

Public Transportation

Public transportation is used as much as Mountainline because the town of Morgantown is essentially the whole campus of WVU.

Taxi Cabs

There is a taxi service that runs 24 hours a day. The prices are reasonable, and they are fairly quick to get to your location after you call.

Yellow Cab Co.

(304) 292-7441

Car Rentals

Avis
local: (304) 291-5867
national: (800) 831-2847
www.avis.com

Enterprise
local: (304) 292-2333
national: (800) 736-8222
www.enterprise.com

Hertz
local: (304) 296-2331
national: (800) 654-3131
www.hertz.com

Best Ways to Get Around Town

The best way to get around downtown is on foot. Everything is close enough to walk to, so there is really no need for a car. The PRT is the easiest way to get from one side of the campus to the other. Buses don't always run on a convenient schedule.

Ways to Get Out of Town:

Airlines Serving Morgantown

US Airways
(800) 428-4322
www.usairways.com

Airport

Morgantown Municipal Airport

How to Get To the Airport

Take Patteson Drive through four traffic lights to WV-705. Patteson Drive turns into WV-705. From WV-705, take a left onto US-119. Take a right onto Hartman Run Rd./ CR-857. Take a left into Hart Field Rd. The whole trip is about six or seven minutes.

A cab ride to the airport costs approximately $5.

Greyhound

Morgantown Bus Station
510 Monongahela Blvd.
Morgantown, WV 26505

(304) 598-2910

Amtrak

There is not an Amtrak station in Morgantown. The closest station is in Connellsville, PA which is about 35 minutes away. Leaving from there will usually require a transfer somewhere along the trip. The other good place to take a train from would be Pittsburgh, which is about 75 minutes from Morgantown.

Travel Agents

AAA Travel Agency

6520 Mall Road

Morgantown Commons

(304) 983-6480

(Travel Agents, continued)

Morgantown Travel Service
Hotel Morgantown SA
127 High Street
(304) 292-8471

National Travel Inc.
3 Suburban Court
Morgantown
(304) 598-0160

Suncrest Travel Inc.
235 High Street
(304) 292-8738

Travel Network
2995 University Avenue
(304) 598-7777

Your Travel-Link
276 Walnut Street
(304) 292-2239

Students Speak Out On...
Transportation

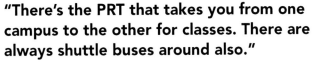

"There's the PRT that takes you from one campus to the other for classes. There are always shuttle buses around also."

Q "Public transportation is not very convenient. **It would be impossible without the PRT**."

Q "The Mountainline takes you to places like the mall and the wharf district for **free with your student ID**."

Q "**Public transportation is decent** when it comes to getting around campus."

Q "**I love the PRT; it is good to ride** and a cool place to be. You can make new friends there."

Q "Public transportation is pretty convenient. **There are bus stops all over**."

Q "With the PRT, transportation is very good, but when that closes down, you really can't get anywhere unless you want to **wait an hour for a bus**."

Q "The PRT sucks! **It always breaks down**!"

The College Prowler Take On...
Transportation

There are two WVU campuses that are separated by about two or three miles. Evansdale campus is closer to the medical buildings and engineering classes, while the Downtown Campus is home to pretty much every other major. The PRT is a great way for students to travel from campus to campus because it is free, and at most, a 20-minute ride from one campus to the other. WVU also has its own busing service that runs from the medical buildings to Evansdale and the to Downtown campus all day long. This is free to students, and the buses usually come every 40 minutes. For students wishing to get to the mall or movies, they can take the Mountainline. This is another shuttle service free to students who show their ID. It travels to the mall, to areas downtown, and to Evansdale. This schedule is more staggered, so student's must plan their activities around it.

For weekends and parties, there is the infamous WVU Drunk Bus. This is basically the same bus service that runs from Downtown to Evansdale, but it runs for hours extended until about 3 a.m. It is used mostly by students who have been out partying. For those who live on the Downtown Campus, transportation really isn't needed because everything is within walking distance except for a grocery store or a mall. To substitute for that, there are several convenience stores and shops in town for students to get the necessities.

B

The College Prowler® Grade on

Transportation: B

A high grade for Transportation indicates that campus buses, public buses, cabs, and rental cars are readily-available and affordable. Other determining factors include proximity to an airport and the necessity of transportation.

Weather

The Lowdown On...
Weather

Average Temperature:

Fall:	50.2 °F
Winter:	37.2 °F
Spring:	56.0 °F
Summer:	73.3 °F

Average Precipitation:

Fall:	9.75 in.
Winter:	9.41 in.
Spring:	11.90 in.
Summer:	12.24 in.

Students Speak Out On...
Weather

{ **"It usually gets cold here around November and doesn't start to warm up again until the middle of April. When it does get cold, though, make sure you have really warm clothes."**

Q "The weather, for the most part, is very rainy. During the summer, the weather is pretty warm for the first few months of school, and **during the winter, you must dress warm**. Be ready for snow and ice."

Q "Usually, the weather isn't too bad. It is in the 40s and 50s in the fall. **Summer can be pretty hot**, and spring warms up a little bit, too."

Q "**The weather here is very mysterious**. The beginning of the fall semester is very warm, and the dorms get very hot, as well. Before you know it, though, it is cold."

Q "The spring semester should be called the winter semester because most of the days are brutally cold. **Warm clothes are definitely needed**, as well as a good pair of snow boots."

Q "The winter months are freezing, and you should wear layers. **Spring and fall are really nice**."

Q "Plan on hot summers and very cold winters, as well as a lot of rain and snow! There are really nice days, but then again, **it does rain a lot here**."

The College Prowler Take On...
Weather

The weather in West Virginia can be beautiful at times and terrible at others depending upon the season. There are definitely four seasons in WV, with summer and fall being the nicest times of the year. The summers are usually nice and warm with constant sunshine and the occasional rain shower. The fall is cool and crisp, and it creates great scenery when all the leaves start to change. The spring and winter are different stories, however. The spring can be a little cold, and it's usually marred with rain. The winter is the most brutal season, however, as it starts in mid-November and extends all the way until March sometimes. Students are pelted with very cold temperatures, snow, and rain, making for an unpleasant time outside.

Students should pack clothes that can be worn in every season. It is especially important for students to bring clothes for hot weather, as well as layers and warm clothes for the extremely cold winters. Rain and snow gear is also very important. Cold weather and rain can put a damper on students' attitudes because it can get so dreary, but the warm weather and nice scenery can help make up for it. One good thing about the winter weather is the great skiing and snowboarding that is available not far from campus. Students can get great rates and even rent equipment from the Student Rec Center. Another bad winter perk: every once in a while, classes are cancelled if the weather is inclement. This is a rare occurrence, yet can happen if a bad enough storm hits.

The College Prowler® Grade on
Weather: C

A high Weather grade designates that temperatures are mild and rarely reach extremes, that the campus tends to be sunny rather than rainy, and that weather is fairly consistent rather than unpredictable.

Report Card Summary

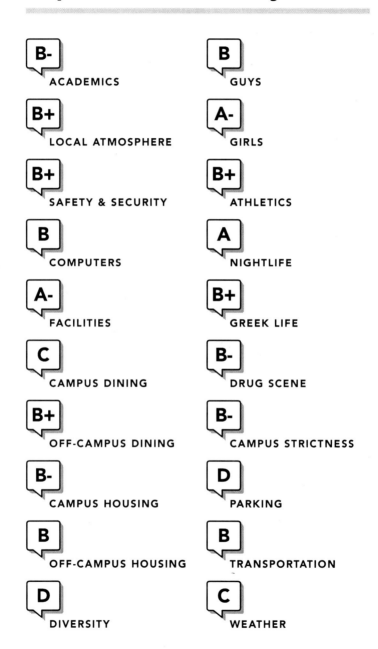

B-
ACADEMICS

B
GUYS

B+
LOCAL ATMOSPHERE

A-
GIRLS

B+
SAFETY & SECURITY

B+
ATHLETICS

B
COMPUTERS

A
NIGHTLIFE

A-
FACILITIES

B+
GREEK LIFE

C
CAMPUS DINING

B-
DRUG SCENE

B+
OFF-CAMPUS DINING

B-
CAMPUS STRICTNESS

B-
CAMPUS HOUSING

D
PARKING

B
OFF-CAMPUS HOUSING

B
TRANSPORTATION

D
DIVERSITY

C
WEATHER

Overall Experience

Students Speak Out On...
Overall Experience

{ **"I have loved my entire college experience so far."**

Q "Sometimes, it would be nice to be closer to home, but it's worth it to be here because **I think I'm getting a great education**."

Q "I have enjoyed my experience at WVU so far. **I enjoy the campus and the atmosphere** of a country school. I am definitely glad I go here. The great social scene doesn't hurt, either."

Q "I like this school. **It is a lot of fun**, and I am learning a lot, too."

Q "I love WVU. **I wouldn't go anywhere else**."

Q "Overall, **I love WVU**."

Q "**I cannot complain about anything**. College is supposed to be the best years of your life, and WVU is making it happen."

The College Prowler Take On...
Overall Experience

Overall, students have made it pretty clear that they are really enjoying their time at WVU. Looking back through this book, it can be seen that WVU has garnered many high grades for subjects such as social scene, academics, and athletics. It is clear that there are many things the school excels in. The aforementioned are huge parts of campus life at WVU, and the students have said nothing but good things about them. While there were many high grades, there were a few grades that show the University could still improve in certain areas. It is clear that the campus dining services are not doing a great job pleasing the students, nor is the parking situation on campus. Considering these are two pretty important things on a college campus, the University should quickly take the right steps to move those two issues into a positive direction.

The attitude at WVU seems pretty split between academics and social events. While most students attend WVU with the expectation of a great education, there are a select few who come to WVU because of the potential party scene. Either way, WVU offers something for each side. With each incoming class comes the promise to improve upon faults and provide students with the best possible experience and education. The athletics program is on the rise and on the verge of gaining national prominence. The academic programs are showing promise as more WVU graduates are gaining recognition for their accomplishments. WVU is a student-oriented university, and should be considered by incoming freshmen who want to be treated to a great college education and experience.

The Inside Scoop

The Lowdown On...
The Inside Scoop

Things I Wish I Knew Before Coming to WVU:

- What a Mountaineer is.

- Where the bookstores are: there is one bookstore in Towers and one right next to the Mountainlair.

- Culture change: Morgantown is less industrialized than other big cities. The culture change can be difficult for some people who come from urban areas.

- Meeting roommates: It is difficult coming to a new school and living with someone in a dorm whom you have never met. Its nice to have more contact with them before moving in together.

- Campus familiarity: getting to know what WVU's campuses are like and what they have to offer before coming here is a huge advantage.

Tips to Succeed at WVU

The biggest tip for succeeding at a school like WVU is to make sure you get your academics on track right away. There will always be chances to go to parties, but there aren't always chances to succeed in classes. Also, get involved with a bunch of organizations. Even going to football games or other sporting events helps build a sense of camaraderie. Lastly, meet lots of new people and make a lot of friends. The key to college is staying happy and stress free, and with the company of good people, it is easy to do so.

WVU Urban Legends

One particular urban legend involves the bell tower of Woodburn Hall. It is said that years ago as a senior prank, a bunch of kids led a cow up the stairs of the tower and left it on top with the bell. It is a known fact that cows will go up stairs, but it is virtually impossible to get a cow to go down stairs. No one knows how they got the cow out of the bell tower, and it is still a mystery to this day.

School Spirit

School spirit at WVU is one of the main things that makes this school what it is. Students here love their school and their sports teams, and they are not afraid to show their appreciation for them. The student sections for football and basketball games are always completely full, and around campus, students can always be seen donning their WVU apparel.

Traditions

One of the better traditions involves the WVU mascot, the Mountaineer. It is tradition for him to shoot off his musket during athletic events when a team scores, or to lead the team out onto the field. This is usually the signal for the students to get loud and crazy. Another big tradition is Mountaineer Week. During this week, various activities occur that show what the state of West Virginia is like. There are crafts, folk music players, a beard growing contest, and a contest to see how many students can fit into a PRT car. This usually garners a lot of attention for students, and it's a great time for all.

Finding a Job or Internship

The Lowdown On...
Finding a Job or Internship

Finding an internship starts with your advisor. They are the initial source to go to when looking to find the best internship. Several schools have their own internship advisor that you can talk to, as well. Depending on your major, there are a lot of places around Morgantown where you can actually take part in your internship. You can also do it in your hometown if you do not live in Morgantown. Internships count for no more than three credit hours and must be discussed with your advisor in order to get the class credit.

Advice

It's never too early to start looking for an internship, and you can do as many as you want, even though you can only get class credit for one. The best time to do an internship is your junior or senior year because you are starting to get into your core classes and have enough knowledge to start and head out into the field. You want to find an internship where you actually get to participate and not where you are just a gopher. This is where your advisor or internship instructor comes in. They can help place you in the best position possible so you get the most out of your experience.

Career Center Resources & Services

www.wvu.edu/~careersc/index.html

The Career Center can do everything—help students find part time jobs and internships, help with resume writing, and search for the best jobs. Appointments can be made to speak with an advisor and get the help you need to get your career in the right track.

Average Salary Information

The average salary for a West Virginia graduate is about $41,000 and is on the rise. In-state, the average salary is much lower than out-of-state, which is giving worry that more and more graduates may leave the state to look for better paying jobs elsewhere. Wherever the job is, however, it is very apparent the WVU graduates are doing well for themselves.

Firms That Most Frequently Hire Graduates

Enterprise Rent-A-Car, Price Waterhouse Coopers, Disney World, PPG, USX, DOW Chemical, General Electric, Exxon/Mobil, Northwestern Mutual

Grads Who Enter the Job Market Within

6 Months: 86%

1 Year: 90%

2 Years: 92%

Alumni

The Lowdown On...
Alumni

Web Site:

www.alumni.wvu.edu

Office:

WVU Alumni Association
Erickson Alumni Center
Fine Arts Drive
PO Box 4269
Morgantown, WV 26504-
4269

Services Available:

WVU Alumni Association
affinity credit card, Insurance
Programs, State License
Plates, WVU Alumni Ring.
For other services check
out *alumni.wvu.edu/pages/
products.html.*

Major Alumni Events

Homecoming Weekend, various chapter meetings; check Web site for upcoming events at *http://calendar.wvu.edu/alumni*

Alumni Publications

WVU Alumni Magazine

Did You Know?

Famous WVU Alumni

Marc Bulger (Class of '99) - St. Louis Rams quarterback

Major Harris (Class of '98) - Star quarterback and Heisman finalist

Donn Knotts (Class of '48) - Actor, was Barney Fife on the *Andy Griffith Show*, the landlord on *Three's Company*, and numerous other roles

Jerry West (Class of '60) - Played for the NBA Lakers, and then was an executive of the Lakers

Student Organizations

- There are over 258 student organizations including honor societies, religious organizations, minority and international student organizations, and many other organizations.

- The Mountaineer Maniacs are one of the biggest student organizations on campus. Students pay $15 to be a member and get a yellow Maniacs T-shirt. They have guaranteed seating to all sporting events, as well as discounts to away games.

- Sample organizations include: American Society of Interior Designers; Bisexual Gay, Lesbian, and Transgendered Mountaineers; Boreman Hall Community Service Club; Brazilian Association; Chinese Students and Scholars Association; Diversity in Media Association; Entrepreneurial Club; Female Equality Movement; Habitat for Humanity; Juggling Club; Moot Court Board; Mountaineer Maniacs; Mountaineer Paintball Club; Muslim Student Association; Mu Tau (Medical Honorary); Veterans of WVU; WVU Democratic Law Caucus; and Young Democrats of WVU.

The Best & Worst

The Ten BEST Things About WVU

1	Party scene
2	Mountaineer football games
3	People/friends
4	Rec Center
5	Up All Night
6	Christmas lights on Woodburn Hall
7	Library
8	Quality of education
9	Drunk Bus
10	Facilities

The Ten **WORST** Things About WVU

1 Traffic

2 Hills

3 PRT always breaking down

4 Dining hall food

5 Parking

6 Cold weather

7 Sorority girls

8 Campus being split up

9 Fraternity guys

10 Out-of-state tuition compared to in-state tuition

Visiting

The Lowdown On...
Visiting

Hotel Information:

There are several hotels around in Morgantown that surround the campus of WVU. Some of the more popular ones are:

Hampton Inn

1053 Van Voohris Road

(304) 599-1200

Distance from Campus:
0.59 miles

Price Range: From $108

Holiday Inn

1400 Saratoga Avenue

(304) 599-1680

Distance from Campus:
1.91 miles

Price Range: From $94

Ramada Inn

20 Scott Avenue

(304) 296-3431

Distance from Campus:
0.59 miles

Price Range: From $79

Take a Campus Virtual Tour

www.wvu.edu/virtualtour

Campus Tours

A student can come on a special Mountaineer Day to see the campus. These days require reservations made in advance because they fill up quickly. Fees are $10 per student and $5 per guest. For more information, call (304) 293-2264. Special tours can also be schedule with the Visitor's Resource Center. These can be for the whole campus, or just specific departments of the University. For more information, call (304) 293-3489 or visit *www.ia.wvu.edu/vrc*.

Overnight Visits

Overnight visits can also be arranged through the same offices as campus tours. Calling either of the numbers above can help to schedule a tour that accommodates you and your family.

Directions to Campus

Driving from the North

- Follow I-76 West (Pennsylvania Turnpike) until you see signs for I-81 South just outside of Harrisburg, PA.

- Pick up I-81 South and follow it to I-70 West in Hagerstown, MD.

- Follow I-70 West until you see signs for I-68 West outside of Hancock, MD.

- Take I-68 West until you see signs for Exit #1, the University Avenue exit.

- After exiting at University Avenue, go to the end of the exit ramp and take a left on to Route 119 North.

- University Avenue will take you right into Downtown Campus.

Driving from the South

- Take I-70 West near Frederick, MD.

- Take I-70 West until you see signs for I-68 West outside of Hancock, MD.

- Take I-68 West toward Morgantown, WV.

- Get off I-68 West at exit #1, which is the University Avenue exit.

- At the end of the exit ramp, turn left on to Rt. 119N.

- University Avenue will take you right into Downtown Campus.

Driving from the East

- I-495 North until you see signs for I-270 West.

- Take I-270 West toward Frederick, MD. At Frederick pick up I-70 West.

- Take I-70 West until you see signs for I-68 West outside of Hancock, MD.

- Take I-68 West and follow toward Morgantown, WV.

- Get off I-68 West at exit #1, which is the University Avenue exit.

- At the end of the exit ramp, turn left on to Rt. 119N.

- University Avenue takes you right into Downtown Campus.

Driving from the West

- Take I-70 East until you see signs for I-79 South just outside of Washington, PA.

- Take I-79 South toward Morgantown, WV.

- Stay on I-79 South into West Virginia until you see signs for I-68. (NOTE: you will see signs for WVU to Morgantown prior to seeing signs for I-68. DO NOT EXIT UNTIL seeing I-68).

- Take I-68 and exit at Exit #1 which is the University Avenue Exit.

- University Avenue will take you right into Downtown campus.

Words to Know

Academic Probation – A suspension imposed on a student if he or she fails to keep up with the school's minimum academic requirements. Those unable to improve their grades after receiving this warning can face dismissal.

Beer Pong/Beirut – A drinking game involving cups of beer arranged in a pyramid shape on each side of a table. The goal is to get a ping pong ball into one of the opponent's cups by throwing the ball or hitting it with a paddle. If the ball lands in a cup, the opponent is required to drink the beer.

Bid – An invitation from a fraternity or sorority to 'pledge' (join) that specific house.

Blue-Light Phone – Brightly-colored phone posts with a blue light bulb on top. These phones exist for security purposes and are located at various outside locations around most campuses. In an emergency, a student can pick up one of these phones (free of charge) to connect with campus police or a security escort.

Campus Police – Police who are specifically assigned to a given institution. Campus police are typically not regular city officers; they are employed by the university in a full-time capacity.

Club Sports – A level of sports that falls somewhere between varsity and intramural. If a student is unable to commit to a varsity team but has a lot of passion for athletics, a club sport could be a better, less intense option. Even less demanding, intramural (IM) sports often involve no traveling and considerably less time.

Cocaine – An illegal drug. Also known as "coke" or "blow," cocaine often resembles a white crystalline or powdery substance. It is highly addictive and dangerous.

Common Application – An application with which students can apply to multiple schools.

Course Registration – The period of official class selection for the upcoming quarter or semester. Prior to registration, it is best to prepare several back-up courses in case a particular class becomes full. If a course is full, students can place themselves on the waitlist, although this still does not guarantee entry.

Division Athletics – Athletic classifications range from Division I to Division III. Division IA is the most competitive, while Division III is considered to be the least competitive.

Dorm – A dorm (or dormitory) is an on-campus housing facility. Dorms can provide a range of options from suite-style rooms to more communal options that include shared bathrooms. Most first-year students live in dorms. Some upperclassmen who wish to stay on campus also choose this option.

Early Action – An application option with which a student can apply to a school and receive an early acceptance response without a binding commitment. This system is becoming less and less available.

Early Decision – An application option that students should use only if they are certain they plan to attend the school in question. If a student applies using the early decision option and is admitted, he or she is required and bound to attend that university. Admission rates are usually higher among students who apply through early decision, as the student is clearly indicating that the school is his or her first choice.

Ecstasy – An illegal drug. Also known as "E" or "X," ecstasy looks like a pill and most resembles an aspirin. Considered a party drug, ecstasy is very dangerous and can be deadly.

Ethernet – An extremely fast Internet connection available in most university-owned residence halls. To use an Ethernet connection properly, a student will need a network card and cable for his or her computer.

Fake ID – A counterfeit identification card that contains false information. Most commonly, students get fake IDs with altered birthdates so that they appear to be older than 21 (and therefore of legal drinking age). Even though it is illegal, many college students have fake IDs in hopes of purchasing alcohol or getting into bars.

Frosh – Slang for "freshman" or "freshmen."

Hazing – Initiation rituals administered by some fraternities or sororities as part of the pledging process. Many universities have outlawed hazing due to its degrading, and sometimes dangerous, nature.

Intramurals (IMs) – A popular, and usually free, sport league in which students create teams and compete against one another. These sports vary in competitiveness and can include a range of activities—everything from billiards to water polo. IM sports are a great way to meet people with similar interests.

Keg – Officially called a half-barrel, a keg contains roughly 200 12-ounce servings of beer.

LSD – An illegal drug, also known as acid, this hallucinogenic drug most commonly resembles a tab of paper.

Marijuana – An illegal drug, also known as weed or pot; along with alcohol, marijuana is one of the most commonly-found drugs on campuses across the country.

Major –The focal point of a student's college studies; a specific topic that is studied for a degree. Examples of majors include physics, English, history, computer science, economics, business, and music. Many students decide on a specific major before arriving on campus, while others are simply "undecided" until declaring a major. Those who are extremely interested in two areas can also choose to double major.

Meal Block – The equivalent of one meal. Students on a meal plan usually receive a fixed number of meals per week. Each meal, or "block," can be redeemed at the school's dining facilities in place of cash. Often, a student's weekly allotment of meal blocks will be forfeited if not used.

Minor – An additional focal point in a student's education. Often serving as a complement or addition to a student's main area of focus, a minor has fewer requirements and prerequisites to fulfill than a major. Minors are not required for graduation from most schools; however some students who want to explore many different interests choose to pursue both a major and a minor.

Mushrooms – An illegal drug. Also known as "'shrooms," this drug resembles regular mushrooms but is extremely hallucinogenic.

Off-Campus Housing – Housing from a particular landlord or rental group that is not affiliated with the university. Depending on the college, off-campus housing can range from extremely popular to non-existent. Students who choose to live off campus are typically given more freedom, but they also have to deal with possible subletting scenarios, furniture, bills, and other issues. In addition to these factors, rental prices and distance often affect a student's decision to move off campus.

Office Hours – Time that teachers set aside for students who have questions about coursework. Office hours are a good forum for students to go over any problems and to show interest in the subject material.

Pledging – The early phase of joining a fraternity or sorority, pledging takes place after a student has gone through rush and received a bid. Pledging usually lasts between one and two semesters. Once the pledging period is complete and a particular student has done everything that is required to become a member, that student is considered a brother or sister. If a fraternity or a sorority would decide to "haze" a group of students, this initiation would take place during the pledging period.

Private Institution – A school that does not use tax revenue to subsidize education costs. Private schools typically cost more than public schools and are usually smaller.

Prof – Slang for "professor."

Public Institution – A school that uses tax revenue to subsidize education costs. Public schools are often a good value for in-state residents and tend to be larger than most private colleges.

Quarter System (or Trimester System) – A type of academic calendar system. In this setup, students take classes for three academic periods. The first quarter usually starts in late September or early October and concludes right before Christmas. The second quarter usually starts around early to mid–January and finishes up around March or April. The last academic quarter, or "third quarter," usually starts in late March or early April and finishes up in late May or Mid-June. The fourth quarter is summer. The major difference between the quarter system and semester system is that students take more, less comprehensive courses under the quarter calendar.

RA (Resident Assistant) – A student leader who is assigned to a particular floor in a dormitory in order to help to the other students who live there. An RA's duties include ensuring student safety and providing assistance wherever possible.

Recitation – An extension of a specific course; a review session. Some classes, particularly large lectures, are supplemented with mandatory recitation sessions that provide a relatively personal class setting.

Rolling Admissions – A form of admissions. Most commonly found at public institutions, schools with this type of policy continue to accept students throughout the year until their class sizes are met. For example, some schools begin accepting students as early as December and will continue to do so until April or May.

Room and Board – This figure is typically the combined cost of a university-owned room and a meal plan.

Room Draw/Housing Lottery – A common way to pick on-campus room assignments for the following year. If a student decides to remain in university-owned housing, he or she is assigned a unique number that, along with seniority, is used to determine his or her housing for the next year.

Rush – The period in which students can meet the brothers and sisters of a particular chapter and find out if a given fraternity or sorority is right for them. Rushing a fraternity or a sorority is not a requirement at any school. The goal of rush is to give students who are serious about pledging a feel for what to expect.

Semester System – The most common type of academic calendar system at college campuses. This setup typically includes two semesters in a given school year. The fall semester starts around the end of August or early September and concludes before winter vacation. The spring semester usually starts in mid-January and ends in late April or May.

Student Center/Rec Center/Student Union – A common area on campus that often contains study areas, recreation facilities, and eateries. This building is often a good place to meet up with fellow students; depending on the school, the student center can have a huge role or a non-existent role in campus life.

Student ID – A university-issued photo ID that serves as a student's key to school-related functions. Some schools require students to show these cards in order to get into dorms, libraries, cafeterias, and other facilities. In addition to storing meal plan information, in some cases, a student ID can actually work as a debit card and allow students to purchase things from bookstores or local shops.

Suite – A type of dorm room. Unlike dorms that feature communal bathrooms shared by the entire floor, suites offer bathrooms shared only among the suite. Suite-style dorm rooms can house anywhere from two to ten students.

TA (Teacher's Assistant) – An undergraduate or grad student who helps in some manner with a specific course. In some cases, a TA will teach a class, assist a professor, grade assignments, or conduct office hours.

Undergraduate – A student in the process of studying for his or her bachelor's degree.

ABOUT THE AUTHOR

I'm a broadcast news major at West Virginia University. I hope to go on to graduate and get a job in the field of sports broadcasting or sports journalism. Growing up near Philadelphia, Pennsylvania, where sports tradition is great, it was not hard for me to decide what I wanted to do with my life. Writing and sports are two things I have always loved, so I figured putting them together was something that could make me very happy, as well as something I could be good at. Writing this guidebook was a chance for me to get exposure, as well as give potential students a great idea of what WVU has to offer. I hope it is found to be a fair and accurate portrayal of not only the positive, but the negative aspects of the school as well. Feel free to contact me by e-mail with questions or comments.

Matthew Bretzius
matthewbretzius@collegeprowler.com

California Colleges

California dreamin'?
This book is a must have for you!

CALIFORNIA COLLEGES
7¼" X 10", 762 Pages Paperback
$29.95 Retail
1-59658-501-3

Stanford, UC Berkeley, Caltech—California is home
to some of America's greatest institutes of higher
learning. *California Colleges* gives the lowdown on 24
of the best, side by side, in one prodigious volume.

New England Colleges

Looking for peace in the Northeast?
Pick up this regional guide to New England!

NEW ENGLAND COLLEGES
7¼" X 10", 1015 Pages Paperback
$29.95 Retail
1-59658-504-8

New England is the birthplace of many prestigious universities, and with so many to choose from, picking the right school can be a tough decision. With inside information on over 34 competive Northeastern schools, *New England Colleges* provides the same high-quality information prospective students expect from College Prowler in one all-inclusive, easy-to-use reference.

Schools of the South

Headin' down south? This book will help you find your way to the perfect school!

SCHOOLS OF THE SOUTH
7¼" X 10", 773 Pages Paperback
$29.95 Retail
1-59658-503-X

Southern pride is always strong. Whether it's across town or across state, many Southern students are devoted to their home sweet home. *Schools of the South* offers an honest student perspective on 36 universities available south of the Mason-Dixon.

Untangling
the Ivy League

The ultimate book for everything Ivy!

UNTANGLING THE IVY LEAGUE
7¼" X 10", 567 Pages Paperback
$24.95 Retail
1-59658-500-5

Ivy League students, alumni, admissions officers, and other top insiders get together to tell it like it is. *Untangling the Ivy League* covers every aspect—from admissions and athletics to secret societies and urban legends—of the nation's eight oldest, wealthiest, and most competitive colleges and universities.

Tell Us What Life Is Really Like at Your School!

Have you ever wanted to let people know what your college is really like? Now's your chance to help millions of high school students choose the right college.

Let your voice be heard.

Check out *www.collegeprowler.com* for more info!

Need More Help?

Do you have more questions about this school? Can't find a certain statistic? College Prowler is here to help. We are the best source of college information out there. We have a network of thousands of students who can get the latest information on any school to you ASAP. E-mail us at info@collegeprowler.com with your college-related questions.

E-Mail Us Your College-Related Questions!

Check out *www.collegeprowler.com* for more details.
1-800-290-2682

Write For Us!
Get published! Voice your opinion.

Writing a College Prowler guidebook is both fun and rewarding; our open-ended format allows your own creativity free reign. Our writers have been featured in national newspapers and have seen their names in bookstores across the country. Now is your chance to break into the publishing industry with one of the country's fastest-growing publishers!

Apply now at ***www.collegeprowler.com***

Contact editor@collegeprowler.com or
call 1-800-290-2682 for more details.

Pros and Cons

Still can't figure out if this is the right school for you?
You've already read through this in-depth guide; why not
list the pros and cons? It will really help with narrowing down
your decision and determining whether or not
this school is right for you.

Pros	Cons
....	....
....	....
....	....
....	....
....	....
....	....
....	....
....	....
....	....
....	....
....	....
....	....
....	....

Pros and Cons

Still can't figure out if this is the right school for you?
You've already read through this in-depth guide; why not
list the pros and cons? It will really help with narrowing down
your decision and determining whether or not
this school is right for you.

Pros	Cons
....	....
....	....
....	....
....	....
....	....
....	....
....	....
....	....
....	....
....	....
....	....
....	....
....	....

Notes

....

....

....

....

....

....

....

....

....

....

....

....

....

Notes

....

....

....

....

....

....

....

....

....

....

....

....

....

....

Notes

....

....

....

....

....

....

....

....

....

....

....

....

....

Notes

Notes

....

....

....

....

....

....

....

....

....

....

....

....

....

Notes

....

....

....

....

....

....

....

....

....

....

....

....

....

....

Notes

....

....

....

....

....

....

....

....

....

....

....

....

....

....

Notes

....

....

....

....

....

....

....

....

....

....

....

....

....

Notes

···
···
···
···
···
···
···
···
···
···
···
···
···

Notes

....

....

....

....

....

....

....

....

....

....

....

....

....

Notes

....

....

....

....

....

....

....

....

....

....

....

....

....

Notes

....

....

....

....

....

....

....

....

....

....

....

....

....

....

Notes

....

....

....

....

....

....

....

....

....

....

....

....

....

Notes

....

....

....

....

....

....

....

....

....

....

....

....

....

Notes

....

....

....

....

....

....

....

....

....

....

....

....

....

Notes

Notes

....

....

....

....

....

....

....

....

....

....

....

....

....

Notes

Notes

....

....

....

....

....

....

....

....

....

....

....

....

....

Notes

Notes

....

....

....

....

....

....

....

....

....

....

....

....

....

Notes

....

....

....

....

....

....

....

....

....

....

....

....

....

Notes

....

....

....

....

....

....

....

....

....

....

....

....

....

Notes

....

....

....

....

....

....

....

....

....

....

....

....

....

Notes

....

....

....

....

....

....

....

....

....

....

....

....

....

Notes

Notes

....

....

....

....

....

....

....

....

....

....

....

....

....

Notes

Notes

....

....

....

....

....

....

....

....

....

....

....

....

....

....

Notes

....

....

....

....

....

....

....

....

....

....

....

....

....

Notes

....

....

....

....

....

....

....

....

....

....

....

....

....

Notes

....

....

....

....

....

....

....

....

....

....

....

....

....

....

Notes

....

....

....

....

....

....

....

....

....

....

....

....

....

....

Notes

....

....

....

....

....

....

....

....

....

....

....

....

....

Notes

Notes

....

....

....

....

....

....

....

....

....

....

....

....

....

Notes

....

....

....

....

....

....

....

....

....

....

....

....

....

Notes

Notes

....

....

....

....

....

....

....

....

....

....

....

....

....

Notes

Notes

....

....

....

....

....

....

....

....

....

....

....

....

....

Notes

....

....

....

....

....

....

....

....

....

....

....

....

....

Notes

Notes

....

....

....

....

....

....

....

....

....

....

....

....

....

Notes

....

....

....

....

....

....

....

....

....

....

....

....

....

Notes

....

....

....

....

....

....

....

....

....

....

....

....

....

....

Notes

....

....

....

....

....

....

....

....

....

....

....

....

....

Notes

....

....

....

....

....

....

....

....

....

....

....

....

....

Notes

....

....

....

....

....

....

....

....

....

....

....

....

....

Notes

....

....

....

....

....

....

....

....

....

....

....

....

....

....

Notes

....

....

....

....

....

....

....

....

....

....

....

....

....

Notes

....

....

....

....

....

....

....

....

....

....

....

....

....

Notes

....

....

....

....

....

....

....

....

....

....

....

....

....

....

Notes

....

....

....

....

....

....

....

....

....

....

....

....

....

Notes

....

....

....

....

....

....

....

....

....

....

....

....

....